# THE RUSSIANS and RUTHENIANS IN AMERICA

*Bolsheviks or Brothers?*

BY
JEROME DAVIS
ASSISTANT PROFESSOR IN SOCIOLOGY IN DARTMOUTH COLLEGE

WITH AN INTRODUCTION BY
CHARLES HATCH SEARS

NEW YORK
GEORGE H. DORAN COMPANY

This scarce antiquarian book is included in our special *Legacy Reprint Series.* In the interest of creating a more extensive selection of rare historical book reprints, we have chosen to reproduce this title even though it may possibly have occasional imperfections such as missing and blurred pages, missing text, poor pictures, markings, dark backgrounds and other reproduction issues beyond our control. Because this work is culturally important, we have made it available as a part of our commitment to protecting, preserving and promoting the world's literature.

## TO
## MY MOTHER
**WHOSE LIFE OF SELF-FORGETTING SERVICE
HOLDS THE SECRET WHICH ALONE WILL
SOLVE THE PROBLEM HEREIN PRESENTED**

# INTRODUCTION

The New Americans Series consists of studies of the following racial groups together with a study of the Eastern Orthodox churches:

Albanian and Bulgarian, Armenian and Assyrian-Chaldean, Czecho-Slovak, Greek, Italian, Jewish, Jugo-Slav (Croatian, Serbian, Slovenian), Magyar, Polish, Russian and Ruthenian, or Ukrainian, Spanish (Spaniards) and Portuguese, Syrian.

These studies, made under the auspices of the Interchurch World Movement, were undertaken to show in brief outline the social, economic and religious background, European or Asiatic, of each group and to present the experience—social, economic and religious—of the particular group in America, with special reference to the contact of the given people with religious institutions in America.

It was designed that the studies should be sympathetic but critical.

It is confidently believed that this series will help America to appreciate and appropriate the spiritual wealth represented by the vast body of New Americans, each group having its own peculiar heritage and potentialities; and will lead Christian America, so far as she will lead them, to become a better lover of mankind.

The writer, in each case, is a kinsman or has had direct and intimate relationship with the people, or group of peoples, presented. First hand knowledge and the ability to study and write from a deeply sympathetic and broadly Christian viewpoint were primary conditions in the selection of the authors.

The author of the study of the Russians and Ruthenians was born of missionary parents in Japan and is a Congregational minister. He is a graduate of Oberlin College and Union Theological Seminary and has a Master of Arts degree from Columbia University where he was Gilder Fellow in 1920-21. During the war he was secretary to Sir Wilfred Grenfell of the Labrador Mission and for over two years was with the Young Men's Christian Association in Russia. He speaks and reads Russian. At present he is assistant professor of sociology in Dartmouth College.

These manuscripts are published through the courtesy of the Interchurch World Movement with the coöperative aid of various denominational boards, through the Home Missions Council of America.

At this writing arrangements have been made for the publication of only six of the Series, namely, Czecho-Slovak, Greek, Italian, Magyar, Polish and Russian, but other manuscripts will be published as soon as funds or advanced orders are secured.

A patient review of all manuscripts, together with a checking up of facts and figures, has been made by the Associate Editor, Dr. Frederic A. Gould, to whom we are largely indebted for statistical and verbal accuracy. The editor is responsible for the general plan and scope of the studies and for questions of policy in the execution of this work.

CHARLES HATCH SEARS.

# PREFACE

The great outstanding fact which has been forced upon me as a result of this study has already been expressed by Jane Addams for the immigrant in general: "We still have no method by which to *discover*[1] the Russians, to spiritualize, to understand, to hold intercourse with them and to receive of what they bring."

When we realize that the total number of foreign-born in the United States from all the Russian empire in 1910 exceeded that from any other country except Germany[2] and that in the one year 1913, before the war stopped further immigration, there were admitted to this country over 51,000 Russians alone, we see the colossal challenge presented to us by the Russians and Ruthenians within our own borders. And now, according to varying authorities, there are between 200,000 and 400,000 Russians and 400,000 to 600,000 Ukrainians in the United States.

At the outset let us be clear as to the terms we are using. By Russian, as used in this study, is meant the Great Russian, inhabiting Central Russia, the White Russian, living between Poland and Russia, and the Little Russian, from what was formerly South Russia. By Ruthenians are meant those Little Russians who come from Galicia, Bukowina, and the Carpathian Mountains in Austria Hungary. Strictly speaking racially, all the Little Russians or Ukrainians, whether from Austria or Russia, belong

[1] The italics are mine.
[2] Bulletin of U. S. Census, 1910. (The estimate includes Finland and dependencies of Russia.)

together, but since many of those inhabiting what was formerly a part of Russia have adopted the Greek Orthodox religion and many desire union with Russia, while the Little Russians from Austria Hungary have a decidedly nationalistic feeling and, for the most part, desire independence, it has seemed best to keep this classification.[1] Both Russians and Ruthenians belong to the Eastern Slavic group.

In undertaking a problem of such proportions it has obviously been impossible, within the time assigned me, to make an exhaustive study. Since I do not speak the Ruthenian language, the investigation of Ruthenian groups has necessarily been seriously handicapped. I was forced to accept secondary sources of information, and the small space devoted to the Ruthenians is a matter of regret to me. My chief emphasis for these reasons is centered on the Russians.

My method (as regards the Russians, and as far as possible for the Ruthenians) has been as follows: I have attempted first to go over the printed material already available on the Russians and Ruthenians in America. A partial list of the books, pamphlets and government reports which are available is to be found appended hereto. This list further includes books on a variety of Russian topics, many of which may not have been consulted. I have also incorporated the results of surveys of Russians and immigrants made by others, such as Mr. Cole of Chicago, the Russian Division of the Foreign Language Governmental Information Service Bureau, the Americanization Study of the Carnegie Foundation, the Inter-Racial Council, and others.

In making my personal investigations my plan was to visit the chief city of each district of the Russian Greek Orthodox Church in America. The

---

[1] See the U. S. Immigration Commission's Dictionary of Races, 1911. I have not kept to this classification entirely.

## PREFACE

cities visited were: New York; Brooklyn; Bridgeport and Hartford, Conn.; Boston; Philadelphia, Scranton, Olyphant, Coaldale, Pittsburgh, and Donora, in Pennsylvania; Cleveland; Detroit; Chicago; Minneapolis. I also visited Ansonia, Waterbury, Seymour, and New Haven, Conn.; Braddock and McKees Rocks, Pa.; Akron, Ohio; and Denver. In the states of North Dakota, Washington and California I had special investigations made among the Russians. In each community visited I interviewed the leaders of the various Russian groups. These included any or all of the following: (a) The Russian priests, (b) the Russian consul, (c) the editor of a Russian paper, (d) Russian professional men, (e) Russian workmen or farmers. I also visited where possible: (a) workmen's clubs, (b) Russian Socialist or Communist party headquarters, (c) typical homes of Russian workmen including boarding houses. In some cases I conferred with the following American agencies doing work for Russians or Ruthenians: (a) American churches, (b) Americanization Committees, (c) Industrial or Americanization Y. M. C. A. secretaries, (d) International Institutes of the Y. W. C. A., (e) banks, (f) labor union officials, (g) employers of Russian labor, (h) public hospitals where Russians are treated, (i) U. S. Immigration officers, (j) teachers or experts who have had special contacts with foreigners. Besides this investigation I have personally interviewed Russians imprisoned on Ellis Island and in Hartford. Later with the authorization of the Assistant Secretary of Labor, Mr. Post, I talked with over one hundred other Russians imprisoned by our Federal government in Detroit and Pittsburgh.

The entire subject of Russians and Ruthenians in the United States is so many-sided that it is only fair to say that the present treatment is not satisfactory even to me. It has been my chief concern to look for the facts impartially, and simply to describe conditions as I found them. I feel confident that anyone who makes a similar investigation in an open-minded way will be forced to similar conclusions.

My thanks are due to all the Russian priests who so generously gave of their time in answering questions, as well as to the Russian Protestant preachers and workers. I also want to thank the Foreign Language Governmental Information Service Bureau, now affiliated with the American Red Cross, for their assistance. The Americanization Study of the Carnegie Foundation kindly gave me access to much of their material. Most of all I wish to acknowledge the help of those numberless plain Russian workmen who threw open their little tenement homes in so warm-hearted a way to an entire stranger. To my wife, who spent many hours in helping to complete and edit my manuscript, I am deeply indebted.

J. D.

## CONTENTS

| CHAPTER | | PAGE |
|---|---|---|
| I | IMMIGRATION | 19 |
| | Migrations in the United States | 24 |
| II | ECONOMIC CONDITIONS | 27 |
| III | SOCIAL CONDITIONS | 39 |
| | Social Organizations and Forces | 54 |
| IV | EDUCATIONAL FORCES | 58 |
| | Forces in Assimilation | 65 |
| V | RELIGIOUS CONDITIONS | 75 |
| | Forms of Religious Realignments | 80 |
| | Forms of Religious Approach | 85 |
| | Literature | 88 |
| VI | SPECIAL RELIGIOUS PROBLEMS | 93 |
| | Leadership of Foreign Language Churches | 93 |
| | Foreign Language Training Schools | 99 |
| VII | RELATIONS WITH THE AMERICAN PEOPLE | 104 |
| | Relations with Governmental Authorities | 115 |
| VIII | WHAT OF IT? | 127 |
| | Recommendations | 130 |

## CONTENTS

**APPENDICES**

  A Bibliography . . . . . . . . 139
  B Theological Seminaries . . . . . 148
  C Religious Periodicals: Russian and Ukrainian . . . . . . . . . . 149

**INDEX** . . . . . . . . . . . 151

## ILLUSTRATIONS

| | PAGE |
|---|---|
| The Wife of a "Russian Red" in New Jersey | 32 |
| Turning the Tables on Uncle Sam | 64 |
| Their View of Americanization | 64 |
| A Russian Poster (Detroit, 1920) | 65 |
| Sunday Morning in a Russian Home | 128 |
| The Results of a Raid on a Russian Club by Agents of "Law and Order" | 128 |

# THE RUSSIANS AND RUTHENIANS
IN AMERICA

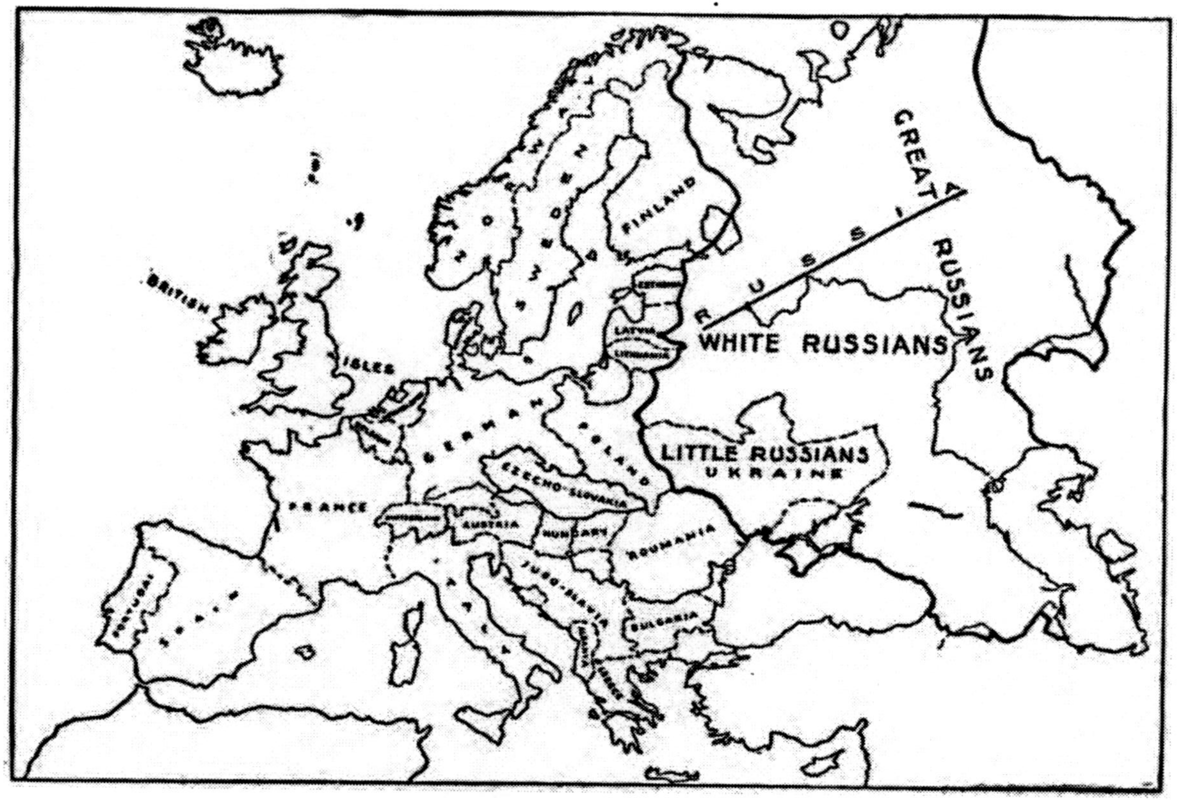
GREAT RUSSIANS
RUSSIA
WHITE RUSSIANS
LITTLE RUSSIANS
UKRAINE
FINLAND
NORWAY
SWEDEN
LATVIA
GERMANY
POLAND
CZECHO-SLOVAKIA
AUSTRIA
HUNGARY
ROUMANIA
JUGO-SLAVIA
BULGARIA
ITALY
FRANCE
SPAIN
PORTUGAL
BRITISH ISLES

# THE RUSSIANS AND RUTHENIANS IN AMERICA

## Chapter I

### IMMIGRATION

**European background.**—The Russian and the Ruthenian come from a dark background of misery, poverty and ignorance. They come from a land but yesterday under the heel of a despot. Education was stifled, the peasants were compelled to live under an oppressive burden of taxation which made poverty almost inevitable, and starvation frequent. They were forced into the maelstrom of wars to become cannon fodder over issues about which they cared little, or not at all. It was thus in the recent World War. Russia mobilized sixteen million men; they were snatched from their homes, to which, during three years of war, they often never returned. They served at a wage of twenty-five cents a month instead of the thirty-three dollars which our soldiers received in France. They ate out of a common dishpan, seven soldiers dipping their wooden spoons into the same bowl for their noon-day meal. There was little or no welfare work done for them; they died like flies. At home their wives struggled alone with the land, accepting without a murmur whatever came of sickness and death; frequently they were entirely without word from their husbands who might be alive or dead for all they knew. Yet in this war they were treated better than in any of the former wars by which Russia has been afflicted. From such a black background have these Ruthenians and Russians come to us. They have been the victims of religious intolerance, class inequality, economic slavery, political despotism, and compulsory ignorance. A fair chance at the good things of life has been denied them.

**Number in America.**—We do not know exactly how many Russians and Ruthenians there are in America. Guesses vary by the hundred thousand. The reason for this is apparent when we consider the complexity of the racial problem involved.

Until 1898 the United States Census classified all who came from territory controlled by the Tsar's government as Russians. From that year on Jews were classified separately, as were also the Ruthenians. In 1910 all who called their native language Russian were considered Russians. When we turn to the last Russian census we find that 2% of the entire European Russian population were Jews who called Russian their native language. Since the great majority of emigrants to America from Russia were Jews, undoubtedly much more than 2% were so included in our census. According to the census of 1910, there were in the United States 57,926 Russians, but 13,781 were Russians from Austria and 1,400 were from Hungary. On the other hand, 3,402 persons were counted as Ruthenians who came out of Russia. Therefore in all, there probably were about 46,147 Russians in the United States in 1910. From July 1, 1910 to June 30, 1919 there has been a net increase of 75,695 Russians over those departing. This would make a total now in the United

States of about 123,000. This, however, does not include the children who have been born on American soil.[1] The Inter-Racial Council and the head of the New York City work for foreigners of the Y. M. C. A. estimate that there are at least 400,000 Russians in America, while Dr. Hourvich, an authority on immigration, places the number below 300,000. Mr. E. I. Omelchenko in his book, *The Financial and Economical Condition of the United States in 1917*, estimates that up to July, 1917, there were 192,920 Russians in this country.

When we turn to the Ruthenians we find the figures even less accurate, since many Ruthenians undoubtedly were formerly classified as Russians or Austrians. From the year 1908, however, the excess of immigration over emigration in the United States has been 139,792. The Inter-Racial Council now estimates that there are 500,000 Ukranians in America, although it states that many Ukranian writers place the figure at 700,000. The Ukranian Alliance of America estimates that there are at least 700,000 and probably many more. These estimates also vary somewhat because of a difference in the racial classifications.

**Distribution and location.**—From Table I below which shows the distribution of the total Russian population in the United States in 1910, we find that New York, Pennsylvania, New Jersey and Illinois are the states having the largest percentage of Russians. New York had 34,612, or 36.5%, Pennsylvania 24,558, or 25.2%, while Illinois had only 4,036, and New Jersey 4,031. According to the 1910 census, then, five-eighths of all the Russians were in New York and Pennsylvania.

[1] The U. S. Census of 1910 recorded 37,211 Russians of foreign or mixed parentage born in this country, and only 25,131 foreign-born and 10,228 native-born Ruthenians.

## TABLE I

### DISTRIBUTION OF RUSSIAN POPULATION IN UNITED STATES IN 1910

| | | | |
|---|---|---|---|
| New York | 34,612 | Virginia | 285 |
| Pennsylvania | 24,558 | Montana | 269 |
| Illinois | 4,036 | Kansas | 260 |
| New Jersey | 4,031 | New Hampshire | 251 |
| Ohio | 3,871 | Rhode Island | 244 |
| Connecticut | 3,013 | South Dakota | 235 |
| Massachusetts | 2,674 | Louisiana | 196 |
| North Dakota | 1,886 | District of Columbia | 189 |
| Maryland | 1,875 | Delaware | 172 |
| California | 1,828 | Maine | 170 |
| Minnesota | 1,517 | Mississippi | 140 |
| Michigan | 1,274 | Kentucky | 134 |
| Missouri | 1,104 | Vermont | 117 |
| Wisconsin | 956 | Alabama | 111 |
| Washington | 666 | Wyoming | 94 |
| Colorado | 546 | South Carolina | 87 |
| Iowa | 511 | Florida | 64 |
| Indiana | 504 | Idaho | 47 |
| Nebraska | 462 | Arkansas | 45 |
| Oklahoma | 389 | Utah | 39 |
| West Virginia | 376 | North Carolina | 31 |
| Texas | 325 | Arizona | 27 |
| Georgia | 299 | New Mexico | 22 |
| Tennessee | 297 | Nevada | 12 |
| Oregon | 289 | | |

By taking the intended future residence of all the Russians who were admitted from 1910-1919, we find that the proportion going to the various states follows fairly closely on the percentage of those already there. During the war, however, there was a shifting of the Russians to the munitions and ship building centers, so that undoubtedly New England now has a higher proportion than in 1910.

M. Vilchur in his book (in the Russian language), *The Russians in America,* published in 1918, gives the figures for the location of Russians substantially as they are given today by the Inter-Racial Council from whom we quote as follows: "New York State 60,000; Illinois 50,000; Massachusetts 40,000; Pennsylvania 35,000; Ohio 45,000; Michigan

# IMMIGRATION

36,000; New Jersey 35,000; Connecticut 20,000. The largest Russian colonies are to be found in the following cities: New York 25,000; Detroit 17,000; Chicago 20,000; San Francisco 15,000; Pittsburgh 14,000; Philadelphia 12,000; Newark 10,000; Jersey City 8,000; Cleveland 5,000; St. Louis 5,000."

Table II below gives the distribution of Ruthenians in the United States in 1910. It shows that Pennsylvania, New York, Ohio, Illinois, and North Dakota each have over 2.5% of the total number of Ruthenians in the United States. Pennsylvania alone, according to the census, had over half the number of Ruthenians living in the entire country. A list of the states in the order of the total Ruthenian population in 1910 follows:

*TABLE II*

### DISTRIBUTION OF RUTHENIAN POPULATION IN UNITED STATES IN 1910

| State | Count | State | Count |
|---|---|---|---|
| Pennsylvania | 19,085 | Montana | 46 |
| New York | 4,611 | New Hampshire | 45 |
| New Jersey | 4,477 | South Dakota | 42 |
| Ohio | 1,301 | Colorado | 38 |
| Illinois | 1,299 | Virginia | 36 |
| North Dakota | 1,007 | Maryland | 36 |
| Connecticut | 616 | Texas | 25 |
| Massachusetts | 439 | Tennessee | 23 |
| Missouri | 382 | Mississippi | 20 |
| Indiana | 265 | Oregon | 19 |
| Rhode Island | 226 | Florida | 14 |
| Michigan | 210 | District of Columbia | 12 |
| Wisconsin | 168 | Wyoming | 12 |
| Vermont | 157 | Nebraska | 12 |
| West Virginia | 130 | Oklahoma | 9 |
| Delaware | 121 | Louisiana | 8 |
| Kansas | 109 | Georgia | 7 |
| California | 92 | Kentucky | 6 |
| Washington | 86 | Maine | 2 |
| Minnesota | 80 | North Carolina | 2 |
| Iowa | 62 | | |

The Inter-Racial Council estimates that today "the majority of Ukranians are in New Jersey,

Pennsylvania, Illinois, and Massachusetts. There are 45,000 of them in Chicago, 35,000 in Pittsburgh, 30,000 in Cleveland, 30,000 in Detroit, 25,000 in Jersey City and 20,000 in New York City."

#### MIGRATIONS IN THE UNITED STATES

**Family groups.**—Among both the Russians and the Ruthenians the family groups do not migrate from place to place as easily as do the single men. After talking with over one hundred families in the various cities I have visited, I have found that 85% of them, irrespective of the length of their stay in the United States, had only made one change of residence from one city to another. A family usually gravitates toward a group of their own kind, where they rent a house or an apartment and take in boarders. Hence it is difficult and precarious for them to move. It is only during strike conditions or general unemployment that they take the risk. If the man of the family hears of better work elsewhere, he will sometimes go alone to test it out, sending for the family if everything proves satisfactory.

**Single men.**—The Russians and Ruthenians without families in this country move much more frequently. Some of them have been in as many as eight different states in five years, but this is unusual. Often they do not stay in the same factory very long. The work becomes monotonous and even if they can get nothing easier, they leave to avoid the dull routine of the lowest grade of machine and mine work. In 78 cases of Russian political prisoners in Detroit who came to the United States within the last 14 years, the following facts are significant: only two of these had wives in this country; the average Russian changed his residence 2.2 times in 7 years; 12 out of the 78 cases, or

15%, had made no change in residence since coming to America, showing that the tendency of the Russian is to remain in one place for a considerable period if economic conditions will permit. This may not be typical of the average Russian, but it would seem that Russians who have been arrested or who have become dissatisfied through failure to become adjusted to American ways, certainly move more often than those who have become so adjusted. On the whole, the Ruthenians probably do not migrate as often as the Russians for they have been in this country longer, they have better established colonies, and they have not had as much of the stigma of Bolshevism cast upon them.

**The return movement.**—Taking the U. S. Immigration figures from 1908-1914, the date at which the European war broke out, we find that 35% of the number of Russians and 16% of the Ruthenians that entered the United States did not remain. Of course, during the war and since, the emigration figures have no significance as an indication of the permanent trend, we have used only the statistics up to the war. The results of the World War, especially the Bolshevik cataclysm and the uncertainty as to the independence of the Ukraine which would take in the Ruthenians, makes it extremely problematical to predict what will happen in the next few years in immigration and emigration. Nevertheless there seems to be a general agreement among authorities that in the year 1920 fully 90% of the Russians here would go home if they could. Until the spring of that year the United States government refused to permit Russians to return to Bolshevik Russia. Today the prohibition has been removed but the difficulties in the way of travel are enormous; still the exodus has already begun. All Russians love their native land. They have not heard from their relatives, their wives and families for three years, a revolution has occurred; they want to see for themselves what has happened. In talking to Russian workmen all over America in 1920 I met only a mere handful who did not say they wished to return at once. At the present time many do not have the funds to leave, still others who are more cautious desire to wait until they hear the reports of their friends concerning Russia. Nevertheless, it would seem probable that for the next few years, at any rate, the return movement to Russia will be very large. This fact places a heavy burden on the Christian forces of America: we must stamp the minds and souls of these outgoing thousands with the beautiful rather than the ugly side of our country.

The Ruthenians do not have the same compelling desire to leave America, although thousands of them long to take part in the building of a free native land at home.

A most strategic policy, it seems to me, for each mission board, would be to coöperate with their Home Mission staff in enlisting Russian leaders in this country. Many of them, if really Christianized, and fully trained here would eventually be native missionaries in their own lands spreading the message of friendship and love.

## Chapter II

## ECONOMIC CONDITIONS

**Means of livelihood.**—Russians and Ruthenians are largely employed in the lowest forms of manual labor throughout the mines and factories of America. Definite statistics as to the proportions engaged in the various occupations at the present time are not obtainable. The United States Immigration Commission, however, in 1909 made a study of 507,256 wage-earners in the mines and manufacturing establishments of America which showed 1.6% of the male and 0.9% of the female foreign-born workers to be Russian. In other words there were 6,588 male and 914 female foreign-born Russian workers and 1,299 male and 1,305 female native-born workers of Russian parents. These constituted 1.5% of the total number of workers investigated.

The actual number of Russians found in each industry then (1909) is still indicative of where the greatest number of Russians is employed. Ranking the 21 industries according to the number of Russians found employed in them, the order is as follows:

| Industry | Foreign Born | Native Born |
|---|---|---|
| Coal Mining (Bituminous) | 1853 | 176 |
| Iron and Steel | 1372 | 150 |
| Slaughtering, Meat Packing | 1010 | 324 |
| Clothing | 536 | 555 |
| Wool and Worsted Goods | 527 | 52 |
| Cotton Goods | 471 | 87 |
| Sugar Refining | 372 | 21 |
| Agricultural Implements and Vehicles | 307 | 250 |

| | | |
|---|---|---|
| Cigars and Tobacco | 220 | 180 |
| Leather | 207 | 106 |
| Glass | 147 | 84 |
| Boots and Shoes | 123 | 64 |
| Oil Refining | 103 | 14 |
| Construction Work | 103 | 2 |
| Silk Goods | 70 | 489 |
| Iron, Ore Mining | 24 | 6 |
| Collars, Cuffs, Shirts | 22 | 4 |
| Furniture | 18 | 27 |
| Copper Mining, Smelting | 6 | 17 |
| Gloves | 6 | 2 |
| Silk Dyeing | 5 | — |

Although these statistics record over twice as many foreign-born as native-born Russians, it is significant that in the easier lines of work the second generation predominate away out of proportion to their numbers. Thus, in the clothing trade, there are more native- than foreign-born Russians. It seems to be true in general that the second generation of Russians leave the harder lines of work and shift into the easier. For example, in coal mining there were only 176, in iron and steel 150, and in sugar refining 21, whereas clothing, agricultural implements, leather, glass, boots and shoes, and tobacco showed a very high proportion of the second generation.

The Immigration Commission found only 901 Ruthenians among the total of over half a million workers investigated. The largest number were engaged in coal mining, agricultural implements, cotton goods, and iron and steel.

Another investigation conducted by the U. S. Immigration Commission among 80,000 employees on the Pacific Coast and in the Rocky Mountain States showed that the greatest number of Russians were in the following industries in the order of their importance:[1] steam railway, coal mining, lumber, beet sugar making, canneries, glass, smelting, cement, electric railways, all industries in which the un-

[1] Abstract of Report of Commission, Vol. I, Table 89, p. 467.

## ECONOMIC CONDITIONS

skilled workers predominate. The Russians take the job at the bottom of the ladder. They have the roughest and hardest tasks; as they express it in their native language, they do the "black" work. In Russia the majority have been peasants working on the land. Further statistics from the Immigration Commission show that in the cases of 5,663 male workers their occupations at home were as follows: 68.3% farm labor; 12% general labor; 8.3% manufacturing; 1.7% a trade; and 9.7% miscellaneous. If we take the occupations of Russian immigrants to the United States from 1910-1914 (the outbreak of the World War), we find that 1,666 or about 1% were in professional occupations, 9,321 or about 7% were in skilled occupations, while 76,294 or about 58% were farm laborers and 45,114 or about 34% were unskilled laborers.

On reaching America nearly all these Russians accept the first work they can get, for they are without funds. Jobs are always to be had, but for the ignorant foreigner who cannot speak English they are naturally of the hardest and lowest types. The mines in which labor is most arduous are open to him; the fiery furnaces of our steel mills offer twelve hours' work a day, seven days in the week; possibly the railroads are seeking construction gangs or the factories will welcome feeders for high speed machines. Ordinarily the Russian cannot secure work on a farm, for the Americans prefer Swedish workers. He has no capital to start out for himself, and besides, he prefers to stay in the neighborhood of his own kind. There are some exceptions such as the Russian Stundists, or Baptists, who emigrated to Virginia in 1894 and started a farm colony. Later they learned from a German colonist that it was possible to get 160 acres per settler in North Dakota, so twenty-five families tried the experiment. By 1900 they had been joined by

400 other families and today North Dakota has about 10,000 sectarian Russians. They even have their own little towns, one of which is named Kiev, after the city in Russia. Their venture has become a marked success and today they probably have the best and most prosperous Russian colony of any in America. Besides these agriculturists there are other colonists in Virginia, Ohio, and other states, who have made farming successful. But the big fact remains that the overwhelming majority, both of Russians and Ruthenians, are to be found in the unskilled trades, and it is here that they are most liable to exploitation. The Christian forces of America have yet adequately to minister to the unskilled workers.

**Changes in means of livelihood.**—As showing the actual reasons which forced a change of employment, perhaps the experience of one Russian is worth recounting because it is more or less typical. Ivan arrived in New York with his wife and spent the first month in vainly trying to secure a job while his savings, the product of years, dwindled to nothing. Finally, hearing of work in the textile mills of Lawrence, Massachusetts, he left his wife behind and, thanks to his splendid physique, was given a job in the chemical bleaching department. But the chemicals and the fumes were deadly and two years of this work took their toll of even his rugged physique, he had pains in his chest, and was looking frail. Because he had been able to save a little money, he left the factory and obtained a job in a coal mine. Here the cramped position, the bad air and the coal dust finished what the textile mill had started; Ivan contracted tuberculosis. Again he gave up his position, spent his money on patent medicines and finally went back to his old job in the chemical department at Lawrence at a reduced wage. It was here that he told me his story and ending said, "Russians like bulls. If you put American at my job he die in two years. I am sick now, but have done it for ten years, and now they call me Bolshevik,—Fool! I don't like America." Now although this is not typical of all, the vast majority of Russians do secure the hardest kinds of work and find it exceedingly difficult to better their condition. They say, "Even when we have ability the boss keeps us in the dirty job because the Americans get the preference."

During the war, thousands of Russians and Ruthenians left their old jobs to enter the war industries at higher pay under better working conditions, which indicates that they will change their occupations for the better whenever they have the chance. There is this fact also to be taken into consideration—and it is close to all human nature—most of these distasteful occupations become monotonous; the worker may go from the mine to the steel plant, thence to digging ditches just to give life a little interest. A Russian workman in the Ford factory told me that his wage was good, that the conditions of work were better than in other factories, and yet he could not stand it to stay there permanently. The monotony of the machine was such that he preferred lower pay and harder work occasionally to the deadening routine.

The children of the immigrant naturally turn away from the hard work of their fathers and try to secure something more to their liking. Frequently they will start driving grocery wagons and end as clerks in small stores—they usually keep changing their employment as opportunity offers. Even so, a surprising number fall into the same rut as their fathers. In the coal mine districts, for example, nearly all the children go into coal mining. Dr. Devine in his *Family and Social Work* presents the case of the sub-normal youth, which would apply to many Russian children: "Parental neglect, congestion of population, dirty milk, indigestible food, uncleaned streets, with the resulting contaminated atmosphere, the prevalence of infectious diseases, multiplied temptations to break the law and ordinances regarding the use of the streets for lack of other playground. . . . Let them be followed by employment in dead-end occupations in which there are no educational elements, no serious motives to progress and application, and we make assurance doubly sure that we shall have sub-normal adult workers. Add a twelve-hour day and a seven day week, irregular, casual employment, sub-standard wages, speeding processes which have no regard to human capacities or nervous strains for which the system is unprepared, indecent housing, insanitary conditions both in home and factory, and we have an explanation amply adequate to account for subnormal wage-earners." This would not apply to all the Russian children, however, for several of the Russian priests tell me that fully 50% of them secure positions as clerks.

**Wages.**—The study of the Immigration Commission in 1909 [1] shows that 2,819 foreign-born Russians received an average wage of $2.06 a day; this is three cents below the average of all the foreign-born. The 248 of the second generation received only an average of $1.98, which was 35 cents below the general average of native-born of foreign fathers. This may be partially explained on the supposition that the children of the Russians are younger because Russian immigration is newer. The same study shows that the 323 foreign-born Ruthenians were making only $1.92 a day or six cents less than the Russians. In view of the small number this is probably not a fair estimate.

[1] Abstract of Report of Commission, Vol. I, Table 26, p. 371.

THE WIFE OF A "RUSSIAN RED" IN NEW JERSEY

[See page 124

**RUSSIAN POPULATION OF THE UNITED STATES**

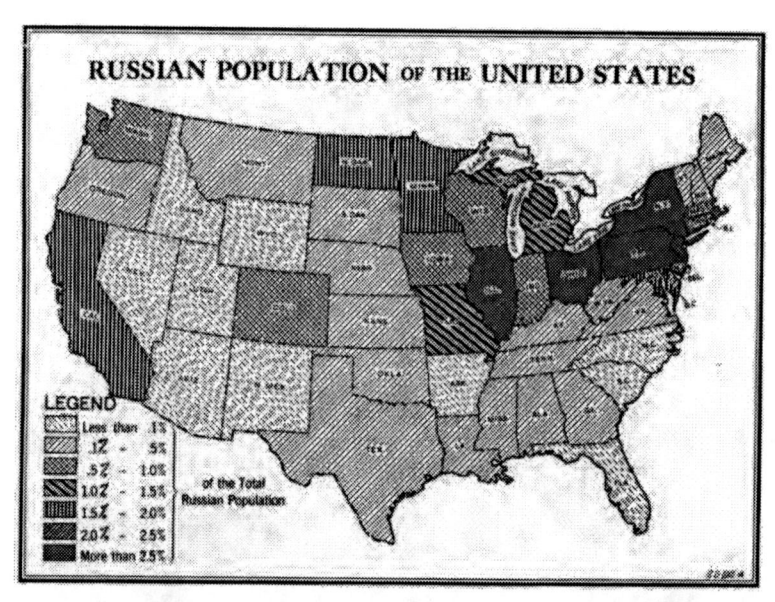

[See page 22]

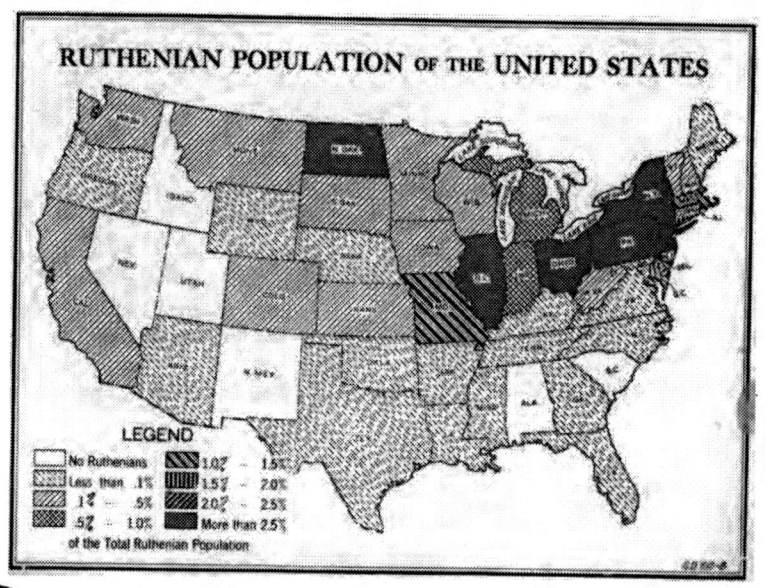

**RUTHENIAN POPULATION OF THE UNITED STATES**

[See page 23]

The war increased wages tremendously; the ordinary Russian or Ruthenian day laborer who had been getting from two to three dollars a day (in Bridgeport, Youngstown, Cleveland, and other centers) during the war reached as high as forty and more cents an hour. But after the war, wages dropped again. A study [1] of 95 single Russians in Chicago revealed the fact that they were making from $12 to $30 a week. The overwhelming majority and the average number earned $23 a week. Of 112 Russians studied in this same report 10, or 9.4%, were out of employment and had been so for from three weeks to four months. They claimed discrimination on account of their nationality.[2] In Pittsburgh in 1920 I found that the average Russian workman received from $25 to $30 a week, but this does not take into account time lost from shut down, sickness and other causes. An average of the wages of the Russians in the cities I have visited would be between $22 to $30 a week.

Standards of living.—Wages are almost meaningless unless we set over against them the needs of the immigrant. How much does his food, clothing and lodging cost? In 1909 according to the Immigration Commission,[3] the average rent paid by the Russian foreign-born was $7.46. The U. S. Labor Department estimates that the average Russian in 1910 spent 101 dollars a year for his apartment. Mr. Cole in his Chicago study found that the greatest number of Russians, and the average, paid a rent between $10 to $13 a month. In the various cities which I visited I found that the rent varied from $10 to $30, but the majority were between ten and seventeen dollars. The second generation tend

[1] M. A. Thesis of J. S. Cole, Chicago, 1919.
[2] *Russki Slovo*, June 5, 1919.
[3] Abstract, Vol. I, Table 65, p. 420.

to pay a higher rent, for they try to make things look more attractive and they demand a better home.

The average single Russian rents a room from a Russian family or other alien; all he desires is a place to sleep and it is immaterial to him how many others share the room, provided the cost is accordingly reduced. He usually secures his board and room in one of the following ways:

(a) By renting a room and boarding himself;
(b) By renting a room and boarding at the restaurants;
(c) By renting rooms coöperatively, eating most of his meals in a restaurant, but taking supper and Sunday meals in their rooms with the others. Often such groups have no system in their buying. First one man makes a purchase, then another, and each time the cost is divided;
(d) By boarding in a family where the landlady does the cooking and the washing. There are several ways of paying for the board. Sometimes, although rarely, there is a flat rate, in which case the landlady keeps no books. In other cases she buys all the food and once every two weeks the total bill is divided. Another method is for the landlady to purchase what each man wants and charge it up in individual account books kept for the purpose.

Everywhere the Russian pays more for the same food than does an American. He patronizes the small stores, run by foreigners, which are in the vicinity of his home. The turnover is not large and the proprietor makes as much as the traffic will bear. Mr. Sibray, the United States Immigration Commissioner in Pittsburgh, told me, "The Russians are receiving good wages today, but the high cost of living takes it all. We charge the foreigner more than we charge ourselves for everything." Increasingly one finds the Russians going into our American shops to buy their groceries. In one place in Pennsylvania, where the mine is three miles from the town, the Russians will walk the entire distance, returning heavily loaded with their purchases rather than patronize the company store which charges higher prices.

The standard of living of the Russian and Ruthenian naturally is low. They are perfectly willing to be overcrowded. In the United States Immigration study in 1909,[1] out of 75 Russian households there was an average of 2.85 persons per sleeping room. Among the Ruthenians, out of 531 households there was an average of 2.83 persons per sleeping room. The general average for the total foreign-born was 2.53, so that Russians and Ruthenians were considerably below the average. In his Chicago report, Mr. Cole recorded the cubic feet of air per Russian in each sleeping room and found that only 35% of the single Russians had the 400 cubic feet required by the Chicago ordinance, and 18% of the family Russians. In spite of this fact, Mr. Cole found that although their average weekly wage was only 23 dollars, 51% were spending 20 dollars or over a week. The Russians buy expensive clothes, and they eat quantities of meat. The daily food ration of the Russian workmen with whom I talked in Pittsburgh was this: at 5 A.M., coffee and bread; at 9 A.M., sausage (culbasa), bread and an apple; at noon, coffee, steak and bread; and at 6 o'clock, cabbage soup, one-half pound of meat, bread and potatoes. The standard of living of the Russians and the Ruthenians seems constantly to be rising. At present they can live more cheaply than Americans only because they are willing to put up with congested quarters and low rents.

[1] Abstract of Report of Commission, Vol. I, Table 72, p. 430.

**The number of producers in the family.**—Nearly all the wives of the foreign-born Russians and Ruthenians do work of some kind. Ordinarily they do their share by taking in boarders. This is not so customary in the case of their married children who have begun to acquire American standards and prefer to be alone. When the foreign-born Russian woman is able to do so, that is, if she has no children or they are old enough, she frequently is also a wage earner. In Hartford the priest informed me that many of the Russian and Ruthenian women worked cutting tobacco in the fields during the summer and in winter received money for stringing the leaves. The children all go to school in accordance with the state laws except that the parents try to evade the legal age limit and force the children to work too early. Even while attending school, the children usually earn some money out of school hours by doing such tasks as selling newspapers, driving grocery wagons and delivering telegrams or messages. The girls often get work in candy and biscuit factories, canneries, and the like. In the rural communities, the children work on the farm and so can legitimately be considered producers.

**Savings.**—Before and during the war, most of the Russian and Ruthenian families were able to save, but there is no accurate method of computing the amount. According to Mr. Vilcher, formerly editor of the *Russki Slovo,* some idea of the extent of their saving can be gained from the fact that the total amount of money sent to Russia by the immigrants, in the few years preceding the war was fifty millions. He also states that 37 workers in one small place sent 47,862 roubles to Russia in one year, an average of about $646 a year. He estimates that in 1917 the average Russian was saving from 20-25 dollars a month; but since the war this has been greatly reduced. Mr. Cole in his Chicago report finds that out of 112 Russians, all of whom had been saving before the war, only twenty are now able to do so. Of 1,138 Russian workmen of the Ford company known to be receiving high wages, 917 had no bank account.[1] In traveling among the Russian colonies I found conditions varying in this respect, but in general, most of the single Russians and Ruthenians who have steady work save something; all of them claiming that it is much less than before the war. This was in large measure due to higher standards of living acquired during the period of high war wages, to increasing costs, and still more, to irregularities of employment. The steel strike exhausted the savings of thousands of Russians, and the fact that the coal miners were working only an average of two hours a day during most of the spring of 1920, also had its effect.

**Unrest.**—The Russian workman feels more of the prevailing unrest than his Ruthenian brother. It is no exaggeration to say that 90% of the Russian workmen are dissatisfied. Setting aside their grounds of dissatisfaction with the American people for treatment in Chapter VII, it seems natural that they should be restless. They feel that they are now getting less wage return in purchasing power than they did when they first came to America. Many of them have given their best health and strength to our industries. Some among them have lost an eye, an arm, or a leg; others have been killed outright in industrial accidents. It seems as if the greater proportion bear the scar of some disaster in industry and all of them bear the scars which come through heavy toil. All this has made for discontent among the Russians. But since the war it has been augmented by the fact that communication with Russia has been broken and many have not

[1] Statistics of the Welfare Department of the Ford plant.

heard from their loved ones in Europe for three long years. A revolution has occurred. The Russian impatiently longs to return to the home-land which he now pictures as the country where all is beautiful, where there is no exploitation, and where the worker has justice. The real cause of this unrest has been well expressed by President Wilson: "It is the human cost of industry, the cost of lives snuffed out, of energies over-taxed and broken, the fearful physical and spiritual cost to the men and women and children upon whom the dead weight and burden of it all has fallen pitilessly the years through. The groans and agony of it all has not reached our ears, the solemn, moving undertone of their lives, coming up out of the mines and factories and out of every home where the struggle has its intimate and familiar seat."

Chapter III

## SOCIAL CONDITIONS

The Russians and Ruthenians in their social relations are almost untouched by American life except for the children who attend the public schools.

**Housing.**—Housing conditions vary according to the colony. In the agricultural districts, most of the Russians and Ruthenians own their own homes. Many of these compare favorably with the houses of Americans. In the mining communities the Russians rent and sometimes buy small houses. In the study of Russian households which was made by the U. S. Immigration Commission in 1909,[1] out of 83 Russians considered, only one owned his own home; and out of 626 Ruthenians only 42 or 6.7%. Since then, however, the percentage has greatly increased. For instance, among 50 Russian families investigated in Los Angeles in 1915, twenty-six owned their own homes, which averaged in value about $2,000.[2] Among the 1,160 Russian employees of the Ford plant at Detroit in 1917, eighteen owned their own homes and two hundred and twenty-nine were buying them. As is usually the case where the tenants are the owners, the houses are in better repair, are cleaner and more sanitary than rented ones, possibly because those who become able to buy are the more progressive foreigners. It is still true today, however, that the great majority do live in

[1] Abstract of Report of Commission, Vol. I, Table 89, p. 467.
[2] *The Russians in Los Angeles*—Lillian Sokaloff.

rented houses. In the cities the Russians and Ruthenians ordinarily rent rooms in tenements. Mr. Cole in his Chicago study of 1919 found that out of 30 occupied by Russians, there was an average of 7.2 individuals living in an average apartment of 4.3 rooms. Eleven of these were front apartments while 14 were rear; one was in the center. Eighteen had their own toilets, eleven had hall toilets shared by 8 to 19 outsiders, and one had the toilet in the yard which was shared by 12 others. Only two of the thirty had a bath tub and in one of these cases it was used for laundry purposes. My study of various Russian communities showed that most Russians are living in the worst type of tenement apartments. The investigation of the 1,160 Russian workers employed at the Ford plant in Detroit in 1917 is one exception. According to the statistics of the Ford investigators 978 had good homes, 157 fair, and 25 poor homes, but the Ford plant naturally attracts the best type of worker. The homes I saw in Pittsburgh are more typical. I well remember one apartment of three rooms. The family was paying $17 a month, but on May 1, 1920, it was to be increased to $20. There was one inside room, entirely without windows and heated by an ill-smelling gas stove, where all the family slept. Five boarders each paid $6 a month for the use of one room, and the other was a kitchen, laundry and living room all in one. I visited two of the steel mill districts and inspected the frame tenements. In one apartment the family, consisting of father and mother and four children, slept in one room, while seven men slept in the other three. All the windows were closed and the floor was used as a spittoon. The rent for the bare, dilapidated rooms without heat was $18 a month. Every crack in the wall was stuffed with rags; a motley array of clothes was hanging in the room to dry, yet this was typical of hundreds of such apartments in Pittsburgh. In general the Russians are at the bottom of the social scale as far as their homes are concerned.

Michael M. Davis, in his study of *Health Standards* of the immigrant, for the Carnegie Americanization Study says, "Wretched and unsanitary housing is not the immigrant's responsibility alone. The native American must bear a large share of the blame." He gives a fair picture of the Russian huts in some of our mining districts: "The coal and iron mining regions of the country to which so many of the Finns and Slavic peoples turn, show some of our worst housing conditions. Shacks are built both by individuals and by mining companies close to mine shafts, pits and coke ovens. Tin cans, tar paper, and old boards furnish building materials for crazy shelters. Into one or more small rooms crowd the large families of the workmen. Toilets are either absent, or else miserable privies are erected and neglected. Out-door pumps furnish water, and the ground surface serves as a sewer." Many of the foreign quarters in our cities are only a step in advance of these. In renting apartments the Russian does not come into contact with the owner but the agent only. It is seldom that repairs are made. As one Russian expressed it to me, "Agent wants money; if ask fix floor he says, 'Go to hell or get out of the place if you don't like it.' "

A typical row of Russian tenements is found on Spruce Alley in Pittsburgh. On one side towers the steel plant, exhaling smoke and dirt twenty-four hours a day, while across the alley live the Russian workers. Frequently the passage is blocked by a long line of empty freight cars waiting to take on their load of steel or to discharge ore. In these small brick houses you will find as many as five Russian families, to say nothing of a score or more of Russian boarders. A typical frame tenement rented by Russians is next to, and above miles and miles of smoking steel furnaces. Garbage and old cans can be seen piled against the fence and upon the sidewalk in front of the house. The little outhouse is shared by all the families in the tenement and one can readily imagine that immoral conditions will result. An apartment in the Soho district is always flooded with water after a hard rain. The fact that the garbage collects in huge piles on each of the three sides and that the little outhouse is the common property of all, creates a sanitary condition beyond description.

After seeing their houses I do not wonder that Dr. John Kulzzyszki, a practicing Ukranian physician in Scranton, told me: "The greatest thing that America can do for the foreigners is to control the renting of houses. Americans build holes which are not fit for pigs to live in and rent them out to Russians. People say the Russians live badly because they live that way in Russia, but there they were compelled to live that way, here they should have a chance to improve their way of living." Perhaps part of the blame for the poor housing may attach to the lack of initiative of the Russians and Ruthenians, but certainly it is to the shame of our social order that little or nothing is done to help educate them to better standards or to compel the American owners to make decency possible for their tenants.

**Health.**—The Russians and Ruthenians coming from an out-door farm life are physically strong, but the change to American conditions is hard for them. Those with whom I have talked give the following reasons why they so often lose their strength in America:

(1) The climate is bad. The damp atmosphere with the alternating hot and cold temperature is far different from the dry cold of Russia.

(2) The factory air surcharged with chemical fumes, dust and other impurities is a radical change from that of the open fields.
(3) The unsanitary tenement houses with the resultant overcrowding breeds disease.
(4) The constant meat diet as contrasted with the fresh vegetables of the Russian peasant is harmful.

As the Orthodox priest expressed it in Coaldale, Pa., "Here they eat bad vegetables, decayed meat and dirty flour." In his opinion the custom acquired in America of sleeping on mattresses simply resulted in a better breeding ground for fleas and bedbugs which were consequently worse than in Russia.

Not only do the Russians eat a large amount of meat, but if they patronize boarding houses they frequently get the worst kind. The wife of the priest in Hartford, Conn., told me she saw one Russian boarding house keeper in 1920 buy 27 pounds of meat for $1.50. It was the cheapest there was for the meat man picked it out from the scraps under the table. Many forces tend to undermine the health of the Russians in America, but fortunately only the strongest and most daring have braved the uncertainty of immigration.

**Recreation.**—Mr. Cole made a tabulation of the predominant recreational interests of 98 Russian men in Chicago, a small sample, but one which corresponds with the author's own investigation. Sixteen claimed the saloon and more than half frequented it; 13 named the movies. The other interests in the order of their importance are: reading 13, dancing 11, music 11, home 6, girls 5, church 5, walking 4, bowling 4, theater 3, pool 3, cards 2 and meetings 2. The men who work seven days a week were very bitter when asked, "What do you do when you want to have a good time?" One said, "When we want a good time, sleep a couple of hours." Another said, "We work like bull, no time for rest."

The Prohibition Amendment has been of enormous benefit to the Russians and Ruthenians, and has brought a change in their recreational life. In one mining town in Pennsylvania the authorities told me that in the days of the saloon they had to keep a special policeman all the time to handle the drunken quarrels arising among the Russians and Ruthenians. Now they have no policeman. Our American civic and religious forces have, as yet, put nothing in the place of the saloon, and the Russian spends his time as best he can. Nearly all patronize the moving picture house. The cases of Russians arrested in the communist raids may be somewhat exceptional and yet they are significant. Out of the 40 interviewed, 18 went to the movies once a week or oftener and to the theater once or more in two weeks. Nine of them went on an average of 2.7 times a week. The remainder went rarely once every two weeks or a month. Those who patronized the movies over twice a week went to the theater about three times a month. If only the religious and civic forces could realize what a potent force the moving picture is! It is so tremendously effective for either good or evil and there is no question about the present evil effects. The foreigners usually patronize the smaller shows. The character of the pictures as seen by the writer were largely of the sex appeal mingled with dime novel mystery and murder. One Russian workman in Akron characterized them as "only play, killing and jumping." Often they depict the life of millionaires living in idleness and luxury. Naturally the Russian who seldom comes into contact with real Americans often forms his conceptions of American life from these pictures. They naturally make him think of the contrast between his family standard and that portrayed in the film.

Card playing is a constant source of amusement. Many of the Russians play at home and often there is the added incentive of money stakes. It is hardly to be wondered at, for when they cannot read they have few other amusements.

Dances are frequently held among the Russian and Ruthenian people and are very largely patronized. Occasionally, also, amateur theatricals are staged. Most of the Russians love music; balilika [1] and stringed orchestras are common.

Until the wholesale arrests by our Federal authorities, many of the Russians attended small political clubs and meetings; since then group meetings have been precarious and consequently secret. It is obvious that for the thousands of Russians working twelve hours a day seven days a week in the steel plants, there can be little recreation. For these men, the first condition necessary is a just change of working hours.

In the agricultural districts the dearth of entertainment is even more apparent. Perhaps it has not been an entire loss that they have not even had the modern brand of moving pictures in so many rural communities. From the foregoing it is apparent that we must provide good recreational centers for these foreigners, if they are to have wholesome recreation at all. The second generation speak and read English and so are able to use and appreciate our libraries and theaters. The amusement problem is not so serious for them.

**Married or single.**—A large majority of Russians are single or do not have their wives with them here.

[1] The balilika is a Russian musical instrument.

In the Immigration report of 1910,[1] 41.4 per cent of the 3,760 Russian males were single, but there were no figures as to how many of the others had their wives in Russia. In the same statistics, 35.1 per cent of the Ruthenians were single. We can be fairly certain that of the others recorded as married, the great majority had wives in Europe. From 1898 until the outbreak of the war, only 14 per cent of the Russian immigration has been female and 86 per cent male. This means that on entering the United States at least 72 per cent of the Russians were single or without their wives.

**Family life.**—Life in such tenements as pictured, page 128, cannot be very ideal. There you see the home of one Russian family. The sitting room, kitchen and bedroom are all in one. The husband works twelve hours a night and when the picture was taken at eleven o'clock Sunday morning, was sound asleep. The three children sleep on the other side of the room. The wife contributes her share toward the support of the family by renting the "extra" room to boarders. The apartment of two rooms costs $16 a month. The condition of the walls can readily be seen in the picture, and it is obvious that in such a house there can be little wholesome family life, yet this is typical of hundreds of Russian homes. The children go to our American schools; their last report cards showed that they were doing good work in their studies but they get no help from their parents who are illiterate. Both these children said they enjoyed school; but as soon as they can pass the school inspector they will be sent to work in order to contribute their share towards the family income. I went over their expenses with the mother and found that the family was not saving a cent.

[1] The U. S. Immigration Commission; Abstract, Vol. I, Table 83, p. 451.

The cost of food, and clothes for the children who insist on being dressed well enough to compare favorably with the other school children, made saving impossible.

This illustration is not typical of all the Russian and Ruthenian families, yet it is surprising how many Russians live in this way. It is even more astonishing how hard some of the women work. For example, Mrs. Sinkovitch in Massachusetts works for 27 people—7 children and 18 boarders. She gets up at six in the morning and works until night preparing three meals daily for the entire group as well as doing all the laundry, yet she thinks she is not working very hard. The pall of hard monotonous labor lies heavy upon the entire family. The men return from the day's work in blast furnace or mine tired out and cannot have any real comradeship with their wives and children. The latter continue to grow away from them: the parents cannot speak English which the children use between themselves, and often even answer their parents in English. Yet I found in many of the homes great pride in the children; the parents want them to secure better jobs and live an easier life than they themselves have had. In many cases, the younger generation grow estranged from their parents because of their backwardness and their old country traits.

**Neighborhood life.**—The neighborhood in which the Russians live is usually the habitat of the Russian Jews and frequently of the Poles, Lithuanians and Ruthenians as well. Outside of business dealings there is little neighborhood life going on. The Social Unit District Plan of Cincinnati would be a wonderful device to help the Russians develop community life. With those speaking other languages, the Russian has little to do. Within the group they go to the Orthodox Church occasionally—more rarely since the revolution—but especially on Easter or for weddings, funerals and the christening of their children. The single Russians have political clubs and some forms of amusement to draw them together. For the women, the store is the rendezvous for information and gossip. It is usually run by one of a Slavic nationality, or by a Jew who can converse in Russian. Of Americans and American life they see almost nothing. Possibly they may attend their children's graduating exercises at the public school, but the chances are that they do not have the proper clothes to wear.

The Ruthenians are much more regular attendants at all church functions than the Russians and in their districts there seems to be more of a neighborhood spirit. Consequently among the Ruthenians the dances, the plays and the neighborhood affairs are more frequent. These obviously are all strictly foreigners' affairs and do not bring the immigrant into touch with American life.

But to children, nationality never means much and immigrant children are no exception to the rule. They need play, and they join heartily with all the others in the neighborhood, regardless of racial distinctions. The ash heap, which is also the garbage and refuse dump, is the playground of a polyglot group of foreign children. The Russians and Ruthenians, along with the little Negroes, slide down the hill on their coats in lieu of a sled. School socials or picnics as well as the class-room work also tend to unite the children. The great need of these foreign children is better playground facilities and the extension of neighborhood settlements with social workers who will show them how to live and work together.

In the rural districts there are very few neighborhood affairs. One of the Russian citizens of Max, North Dakota, told me that until 1915 the Russians feared to get together for anything except religious services; the habitual distrust of generations of a Tsar's tyranny still persisted in the land of free speech and assembly.

**Moral standards.**—The moral standards of the single Russians are comparatively low as regards sexual immorality. The reasons are plain: they are far from their wives, or perhaps are forced to remain single because of the small number of unmarried Russian women in this country. The dark halls, the toilets used in common, and the living arrangements in which men, women and children sleep in close proximity, all make for moral laxity. Furthermore, in the case of a family which takes in boarders, the husband leaves the wife alone with the tenants for long hours at a time; he may even work on a night shift. The Russian newspapers frequently advertise asking for knowledge of the whereabouts of a wife who has run away with one of the family's boarders. In the agricultural districts the moral standards are much higher: there is seldom any crime and there is much less immorality.

In 1908 statistics of alien prisoners in the United States [1] showed 156 Russians imprisoned; of these 41 per cent had been committed for gainful offenses, 25 per cent for personal violence, 25.6 per cent against public policy and only 2.6 per cent against chastity. The latter is about 1 per cent below the total average. Of 119 Russians in charity hospitals in 1909,[2] only 4 had venereal disease and among 30 Ruthenians only 1. Except for so-called political offenses (that is, membership in the Communist Party or sympathy with the Russian Bolsheviks), I found that universally the Russians were considered very law-abiding by the public authorities. This was even more true of the Ruthenians because they did not have the stigma of Bolshevism attached to

[1] Abstract Immigration Commission, Vol. I, Table 36, p. 212.
[2] *Ibid.*, Vol. II, Table 18.

them. The crime statistics as reported by the City of Chicago [1] show that the percentage of Russian criminals out of every 1,000 is far smaller than the corresponding ratio for Americans. Is it not significant that although the Russians were living in the worst section of the city, in touch with the sordid side of American life, they were as law-abiding and as honest as the average American?

**Relation to the old country.**—The second generation of Russians and Ruthenians feel that America is their home. They speak English and understand it better than they do Russian; they have not the same longing to see the old country their parents have. Nevertheless, the unfortunate experience which a few of them have had in our industrial life has embittered them against America—the squalid tenement houses, the daily grind of the factory, the isolation from the good things of American life. These men want to try the new Russia if perchance she will prove to be a land of freedom. Some of the younger Russians who actually want to become citizens meet opposition from their parents who say, "We are only transients in an unfriendly country."

While the Russians and Ruthenians on the farms keep as closely in touch with the homeland as do the others, most of them feel more contented and plan to make America their permanent home.

**Relation to other racial groups.**—The Russians and Ruthenians do not mix together much, although they do inter-marry. One never finds a Russian club with many Ruthenians enrolled and the reverse is also true. The pastor of one of the Protestant Russian churches told me that he found it difficult to get them to mingle at all. He said that irrespective of the differences in the language, they just aren't happy together. Because there is such a dearth of

[1] Annual Report Police Department, Chicago, 1919; Report of the Chicago City Council Committee on Crime, 1915.

Russian women, however, they sometimes intermarry.

The Russian workmen dislike the Irish because so many of the latter, as bosses, treat them badly in the mines and factories. The Orthodox priest in Olyphant, Pa., said, "The Welsh give toward my church work, the Irish say 'get out' and I have not met a real American here." The workmen say the Poles make better bosses than the Irish, but still are bad, and the Americans are better than either, but are seldom met. Of course the Russian meets the other nationalities employed in his shop, and if he is farming, he meets the neighboring farmers, whether Germans, Norwegians, Bohemians or Swedes, and the relationship is usually a friendly one.

All the Slav groups intermingle somewhat and you find some intermarriage between Russians and Poles. The Jews play an important part in the life of the Russians and Ruthenians in this country as many of them speak one or the other of their languages and come from Russia. When the Russians wish to deposit their money, they frequently turn to a Jew; when they are sick, a Jewish doctor prescribes their medicine, and if they are in legal difficulties, a Jewish lawyer helps them out. Indeed, many of the Jews are rendering excellent service to the foreigners. At the same time there are many shyster doctors and lawyers who exploit the ignorant Russian and Ruthenian. The Russian newspapers display in flaring advertisements: "Sick People Come to Me," "Consultation Free," "Hundreds of operations for both men and women have been avoided," "Do you suffer from weak nerves, lame back, pimples, sores, catarrh, sore throat, constipation, etc., etc.," "My principle—the golden rule," "In the treatment of rheumatism, blood and skin disorders and many other ailments, electric treatment, intravenous injection and absorption methods assure you of positive results without interference with your work."

Naturally the methods of the bad Jews have placed a certain amount of stigma on them all. Nevertheless, the Russians and Ruthenians patronize them now, and will continue to as long as they know of no better place to go. The Jewish doctors like their Russian patients. "They always pay our fees without grumbling," is the comment of one such physician. Today a few Russians are beginning to go to American doctors, but most of them dislike to because of the larger fee and the difference in language. One Russian showed me a bright red spray which had been prescribed for him and said, "That comes from a negro doctor, they are better than other Americans, for they charge less." I asked several of the Russians why they didn't go to the free wards. They replied, "We don't care to be experimented on, like dogs and chickens." In telling me why he patronized a Jewish dentist rather than an American, a Russian said, "The American takes only fifteen minutes, says 'Hurry up, Hurry up—get a jump,' the Jew takes an hour and charges same." Another Russian told me that he had a tooth extracted but it proved to be the wrong one, so he went back to the American dentist. "Well, I was busy and didn't know what I was doing," said the dentist, as he pulled the second one. Then he charged him for both teeth. On the whole, the Russians, the Ruthenians and other races have a cordial feeling for each other, but they do not mingle much. The second generation feel more or less their solidarity with Americans and some even marry into American homes, although this is rare. More often they marry the native-born children of some other Slavic race.

**Racial prepossessions and aspirations.**—The Russian and Ruthenian are both thrifty, they try to save money. They are willing to endure any conditions no matter how bad, and will work uncomplainingly for long hours at low wages. Stolidity is inborn. The Russian is markedly religious. In every home you see an ikon or sacred picture. As to the church, he may be skeptical; he is often suspicious of the priest, who, he says, is out for money first. The love of music is a well-known characteristic; the theater is popular also. The Russian is very sympathetic, always willing to contribute to the needs of those who are suffering. If a Russian is killed in the mine or factory, his neighbors will care for the widow and children even though they themselves are barely making both ends meet. The Russian is naturally suspicious of others, the inevitable and bitter result of a long experience under the corrupt officials of the Tsar. None the less, sociability is a marked trait. The Russian likes to talk by the hour to his friends and will share his last morsel of food with a stranger. He is idealistic, generous, quickly responsive to the higher good, and willing to suffer to bring in what he considers an ideal for the common welfare even at great cost to himself. This was well illustrated in the steel strike of 1920. Thousands of Russians used up every cent of their savings, denied themselves the food they needed, suffered the loss of work and imprisonment, all for the general good. Yet some of the men had been drawing very high wages and need not have struck from a desire to better their position. The Russian does not aspire to wealth, but he does want to get away from the work in factory and mine which he hates; he longs to get back on the farm. Those Russians who are in rural work and are making a success of it seem to be contented.

## SOCIAL ORGANIZATIONS AND FORCES

**Destructive.**—There is no outstanding wholly destructive force among the Russians themselves.

Until the United States started its raids there were scores of Russian branches of the Socialist and Communist party scattered over America. Hanging on the wall of one club visited in December, 1919, at Boston, was the certificate of incorporation which read, "Mutual Aid Association of Workmen from Russia for the purpose of paying death or funeral benefits not exceeding two hundred dollars, and disability benefits not exceeding ten dollars per week. The association shall maintain a library and conduct lectures for the purpose of educating its members and also assist them in raising the standard of their living. The membership is limited to persons of Russian birth or descent." The charter was granted by the State of Massachusetts on December 6, 1915.

On the walls were pictures of all the Russian revolutionary leaders, Gorky, Lenin, Trotsky and others. Besides, there was a certificate of membership in the Communist party. The club had both men and women members. They had classes in both Russian and arithmetic. The library had many standard Russian books, besides all the leading Russian daily newspapers. A buffet which served soft drinks actually paid for the rent of the room, which was twenty dollars a month. The club also maintained a school for the children of members which met three times a week. As far as I could judge, although the club included the political, it also met a legitimate social and educational need, and to that extent was constructive. After listening for hours to study classes in the various Communist clubs, I must admit that they do seriously attempt to teach their own members. They have merit in that they do not go over the heads of the illiterate workers. Still, such clubs also have lectures which stimulate Bolshevism, and there is little doubt that part of the propaganda work now going on in the club we have described may have been directed against our political system and American ideals. There are few social agencies other than these, however, and here they were trying to do for themselves what no one else had done for them. Whether or not this club has since been broken up by officers of the Department of Justice, I do not know. I do believe, however, that to destroy such a social club without putting something constructive in its place is but to stimulate Bolshevism.

The saloon was probably the most potent evil among the Russians until its downfall in 1920. Since then perhaps the most deadly agency has been the clever deceivers of the ignorant Russian and Ruthenian. These are not only the communist agitators, but the lying doctors, lawyers, or exploiters of any kind. When a Russian Jew, or any other person, organizes an association to relieve the distress in Russia and pockets the funds, as the Russian priests have cited instances to me, that is a destructive force, for it shatters the faith of the Russian in America. The agitator is constantly preaching to him, "Only the face of America is democratic"; he recounts instances of injustice and unkindness which are just true enough to win over the ignorant Russian. Moreover, the forces of political graft make more strenuous efforts to corrupt the immigrant than the forces of good to Americanize him. Edward A. Steiner, whose experience surely should enable him to speak with authority, writes: "The year I lived in Streator (Ill.) when the Slav had no vote or influence, politics in that city were already corrupt and the corrupters were native

Americans, whose ancestors harked back to the Mayflower and who were rewarded for their corruption by high political offices. The Slav now has some political power; but as yet he has not produced the 'grafter.' I do not say he will not; but when he does, small blame to him."[1]

**Constructive.**—The Russian Church, handicapped as it is (see Chap. V), is one of the big constructive forces in the life of the Russian. The brotherhoods of the church, their insurance societies, are helping the Russian because they are keeping him from suffering in times of disaster. The Russian educational clubs and the little Russian reading rooms which are often started in Russian colonies are constructive. Even the concert and dance, when properly conducted, provide necessary recreation. The educational forces described in the next chapter are making as large a contribution as any. But at best the constructive social forces for the Russian are woefully inadequate.

The Ruthenians have stronger local clubs and societies; they attend their churches regularly. In some places they even have Ukrainian "Homes" or clubs, and consequently have somewhat more than the Russians. The latter especially feel they are aliens, and they need everything that we can do for them in order that they, in turn, may become socially valuable as well as industrially so. Among the children the one big constructive force is the school. The teacher can counteract many handicaps in the home environment, though her sphere is necessarily limited by the number of hours spent each day in school and the economic pressure which puts children to work at the earliest age legally possible.

We have seen that destructive forces assail the Russian on every side, while constructive forces

[1] *Twenty-five Years with the New Immigrant in Immigration and Americanisation,* by Philip Davis.

function so weakly that, as one Russian Protestant pastor said in a statement to me: "Ninety-five per cent of the immigrants do not understand either the Americans or their institutions. They receive their conceptions about America from the hard side. They mingle only with the base elements and from them get their interpretation of America."

## Chapter IV

## EDUCATIONAL FORCES

**The public school.**—In the 1909 investigation of the United States Immigration Commission we find that in only seven out of thirty-two representative cities are there over 200 Russian children enrolled in the public schools. These seven are: Boston, Chicago, Los Angeles, Newark, New York, Philadelphia and Yonkers. Of the total of 4,628 of these children, 285 or 6.1 per cent were in the kindergarten, 3,136 or 67.7 per cent in the primary grades, 988 or 21.3 per cent in the grammar grades, and 219 or only 4.7 per cent in the high school.[1] This is about the same as the total for all the foreign nationalities except that the latter have about 10 per cent larger enrollment in the grammar grades than the Russians. Since the Russian immigration is newer, this may be due to the fact that the children are younger. According to the same authority,[2] in 77 higher educational institutions in the United States there were a total of 27 Russians or .1 per cent of the total number of students. The figures for the Ruthenians in the public schools did not total 200 in any city, so that summaries for them were not given. In the higher educational institutions there was only one Ruthenian. In my investigations I found that generally the Ruthenian and Russian children are attending the public schools in accordance with the laws of the various states. This does not

[1] Abstract of Report of U. S. Immigration Commission, Vol. II, Table 6, p. 24.
[2] *Ibid.*, Table 53, p. 78.

mean to say, however, that some of the parents do not take the children out of school before the law permits when there is lax enforcement. This is done to some extent, particularly among the poorest families. There can be no question but that the public schools are the strongest force for assimilation that we have. Here the children learn of American ideals, they are taught our history and they take part in our flag-drills, which they enjoy. In some of the cities the schools have been turned into social centers with gymnasiums, libraries and clubs, and thus become a still greater force for assimilation.

It is unfortunate that our public schools do not also teach the best that each foreign race has to offer. True Americanism should impart not only the best that our country has, but also the best culture from other civilizations that our own may be enriched with the finest from the rest of the world. For example, we should make the Russian boy feel proud of Russia's great writers, of her musicians and men of science. We should teach him that his racial heritage is such that he, too, should contribute his bit to America, as well as receive.

**Parochial schools.**—The United States Census of Religious Bodies for 1916 shows that the Russian Greek Orthodox Church has 126 schools with 150 officers and teachers and 6,739 students. This makes an average of only one teacher to 45 students and even then, all the officers are counted as teachers which is not the fact. Considering the number of Russians in the United States, 6,739 children seems also to be a rather small proportion of the total number. Unfortunately these schools have not been kept free of politics. They have usually taken an anti-Bolshevik stand, and as a result in some cases the children have been kept at home; in Bronxville, N. Y., the workmen even withdrew their children and started another school of their own. The writer found in visiting the various cities that these parochial schools for Russians did not attempt to take the place of the public schools. They usually met only three times a week after school hours. Many of the priests frankly admitted that the main purpose of the parochial school was to teach the children Russian and to preserve their religious and Russian customs. In the great majority of cases they constitute a force working against assimilation. For example, in the official Russian-American Greek Orthodox Church calendar a picture depicting the history of the United States is included in the section on humor (page 64). This is just the section which the children would be likely to read and certainly this would not add to their love for our country.

The Ruthenians, whose churches are included in the Roman fold, have some schools which attempt to take the place of our public schools. Usually they are not adequately manned with teachers. The purpose of the school is to keep the children loyal to the Catholic faith, but unfortunately, at the same time they also work against Americanization. When the children leave the parochial school they are far behind the other children who have been in the public schools.

**Literature and newspapers.**—Both the Ruthenians and the Russians in this country have a great deal of literature in their native tongue. The Russian bookshops are full of the works of classical writers such as Tolstoy, Turgenieff, Pushkin, Dostoevsky and others. The public libraries of many of our larger cities have a great number of books in Russian and some of them as, for example, the New York Public Library, have a special Slavic department. Many of the better educated Russians and Ruthenians are using these facilities, but the rank and file are hardly touched by them.

On the other hand the Russian and Ruthenian newspapers reach the great majority. At the present time the chief Russian newspapers are the *Russki Slovo*, which takes an anti-Bolshevik stand, and the *Russki Golos*, which is opposed to intervention in Russia and is generally favorable to the Bolsheviks. The *Novi Mir* was suppressed by the government in 1920 for being too Bolshevistic in sympathy.

The Russian Bureau of the Foreign Language Governmental Information Service sent out a letter and questionnaire to Russians in the United States. They received a total of 198 replies of which 84 were from unskilled workers, 48 from skilled workers and mechanics, 13 from farmers, 13 from miners, 9 from ministers, 11 from educational workers and the rest were miscellaneous. In answer to the question, "Do you read English books or newspapers?" 70 replied that they read the newspapers, but that they did so in spite of the fact that they "could hardly understand them." Only three read books and magazines in English. These answers seem highly significant because they come from picked Russians. Any workman who would reply to such a letter must necessarily be literate and many of them are skilled workers. The startling fact is that among these people only three read American magazines and books, and most of those who read English newspapers admit they cannot understand them. On the other hand, the Russian newspapers are read widely. I have often seen in a Communistic club one intelligent Russian worker reading the Russian paper to half a dozen illiterate comrades. All the workmen's clubs carry Russian papers, hence their influence is most widespread. In order that the reader can gather something of the attitude of these papers, let me quote from each of the chief Russian New York papers, including the now suspended *Novi Mir*.

*Novi Mir,* Nov. 21, 1917
(A Translation)
"The Russian immigrant feels lonesome in America."

"He has no friends, and there are no social centers for him through which he can gain friends. It is for this reason that American life to the Russian immigrant seems to be dull and gray. He works, eats and sleeps, and takes a stroll on holidays; but he walks with a sad face and does not seem to enjoy life.

In moments of distress or doubt he has no one to confide in or no one from whom he can secure moral support.

He is exploited by everyone who is not too lazy to take advantage of him—by the banker, by the doctor and by the lawyer charlatan, and by every clever man who knows how to 'fish in muddy water.' He stands alone in the social life—helpless."

*Russki Golos,* April 10, 1920
(A Translation)
"Do you like America?"

" 'If you don't—get out,' says the landlord to his tenant. Masters of American land—they are the landlords too. What they are used to saying to their tenants, they say to the immigrant masses. By their order articles are written in newspapers which are read all over the country. They dictate the words that are shown in brilliant letters on the screen in moving pictures. Every day these words stand before the people's eyes, are whispered in their ears. They poison the soul of the American people with spite and stupid arrogance. These offensive words are daily thrown into the newcomer's

—immigrant's face. 'If you don't like it—get out,' says the landlord to his tenant. 'If you don't like this country—get out,' shout the capitalistic newspapers and moving pictures to the immigrant laborer.

'Get out from here,' is told to the immigrant. These words are not only stupid, they are false. If millions of workmen, who came here from Europe will leave the United States, America's strength and wealth will vanish. In the big theaters among dancing and other entertainments you see these same words on the screen: 'If you don't like this country —get out.' Many would like to get out and will do it as soon as possible. But is it true that we do not like this country? We like this country as any country. Here also the sun shines, the woods murmur and the rivers flow. This country is a good field for human labor. As everywhere else, here are people humiliated by the strong ones. As everywhere else the money bag is ruling.

It is not that we do not like America. We do not like the great amount of violence and falsehood that is in America. We do not like it that in America are stupid people. They are among those who throw in the face of the Russian and European workman, who have helped to create the wealth of America, the offensive words, 'Get out from here.' "

*Russki Slovo,* Dec. 1, 1919
(A Translation)

"In one of the big naphtha factories in Brooklyn, two Russian workmen were discharged only because they talked to other workers during the intermission. The Superintendent decided they were 'dangerous agitators'; in reality, they were calm and quiet and took no part in politics."

*Russki Slovo*, Dec. 24, 1920
(A Translation)

"America is not at all interested in the soul and spiritual life of the Russian immigrant, only in his muscles. He came to this country a stranger and often leaves it again without any American knowing him at all. It is therefore very unjust to accuse him of disloyalty, ingratitude and revolt."

Nearly all these articles would tend to antagonize the reader against the American people and yet for the Russian there is much of justice in the viewpoints. Besides these papers there are the still more radical I. W. W. ones printed in Russian at Chicago such as *The Voice of Labor*. These have daily cartoons which, for example, depict the capitalist as a shark devouring the worker, with the I. W. W. coming to the rescue with direct action.

On the other hand, the newspapers such as the *Russki Slovo* and the *Russki Golos* do print material which would definitely help the foreigner to understand America, but it is almost infinitesimal compared to what it might be if more definite coöperation were given to the newspapers by social and religious agencies. Recently the Inter-Racial Council has, I believe, done something in this direction by buying up advertising space.

**Leadership.**—The leadership of the Ruthenians is pretty largely in the hands of the priests and the heads of local and fraternal organizations. They seem, on the whole, to be very able and capable.

Among the Russians there is such conflicting leadership that as one of their workmen said, "Every Russian his own leader, only Bolsheviks united." Nevertheless, there are certain men who stand out from the others. The priests have been at the head

**TURNING THE TABLES ON UNCLE SAM**
One page from the Humorous Section of the official Russian-American Greek
Orthodox Church calendar.  [See page 60]

**THEIR VIEW OF AMERICANIZATION**
Russian Workers carry banners endorsing both President Wilson and the Soviets in the
Americanization parade in Pittsburgh July 4, 1918.  [See page 129]

A RUSSIAN POSTER (DETROIT 1920)
"Give to the fund for the politically imprisoned."

[See page 93

of their religious groups, but today the rank and file of the Russians do not accept their leadership because they are too conservative. Fully 90 per cent of the Russians in the United States are workmen and they either trust nobody or else they look to those prominent in their workers' clubs. Naturally these men are very sympathetic with the Bolshevik experiment in Russia. They have not been there, but they know it is a workingman's government and they are workingmen. The radical Bolshevik propagandist and the Russian I. W. W. leader consequently exert a good deal of influence among certain numbers of the Russians. These are not always the unthinking; most often they are the men who have become embittered by some harsh experience here. Besides these radical leaders, one usually finds some Russian who through hard work and friendly dealing with his fellow-countrymen has gained prestige. He often lends money to the Russian who has met with misfortune and, more often still, gives advice. The intellectual and professional Russians have lost much of their prestige because, for the most part, they have been such bitter propagandists for Kolchak, Denikine, and the other anti-Bolshevik military leaders. The editors of the various Russian papers probably wield more influence than anyone else today, and next to them come the heads of the various workingmen's clubs, including the heads of the branches of the Communist Party.

### FORCES IN ASSIMILATION

**Agencies.**—The greatest assimilating agency that we have in America is the public school. Jane Addams says that the only service America is thoroughly equipped to offer the immigrant and his children is free education. When we consider that in 1910, according to the census, over one-fourth of the children in our schools were of foreign or mixed parentage, we can imagine something of the service we are rendering the foreigner in this way.

The Y. M. C. A. in its work in the factories and among the foreign-born, has frequently rendered notable service for the Russians and Ruthenians. In this connection the work of Mr. Harvey Anderson in New York, and Mr. Theo. G. Demburg in Philadelphia, has been especially significant. They have organized lectures, classes, and information bureaus for the foreigner, besides coöperating with every other agency in the city.

The Y. W. C. A. in its International Institutes has also been making a big contribution. For example, in Pittsburgh it has an information service with a paid Russian worker. Any Russian or Ruthenian who needs advice or help can receive it there. Besides this, they conduct classes in English right in the factory districts where the Russians live.

The Foreign Language Governmental Information Bureau, organized by the Committee of Public Information of the Government, and now affiliated with the Red Cross, has been giving excellent help as a connecting link between the government and the alien. At first it sent bulletins to the Russian papers giving material relating chiefly to the war; later it began to give information to Russians in general. It interpreted our laws to them and was the means of saving thousands of dollars of income taxes wrongly collected from Russians. It has also translated books on hygiene, technical works, histories of the United States, works on citizenship and historical plays for the free use of foreign language schools, churches and societies. Moreover, it has sent Russian lecturers to all parts of America who speak in Bolshevik clubs, workmen's halls and other meeting places, on such subjects as American Ideals or Abraham Lincoln.

During and since the war, Americanization Committees have had a mushroom growth. While there is no doubt that they have helped the foreigners tremendously, they have not touched the life of the Russian as much as the other nationalities. For example, an investigator of Russian conditions for a department of our government says, "The Pittsburgh Public School authorities are carrying on Americanization campaigns, aided by the Chamber of Commerce, which ever so often invite the 'leaders' of the foreign-born to a dinner. So far as the Russians are concerned the results of this work are invisible." Mr. George Creel, head of the Committee on Public Information of the Government during the war, says,[1] "Americanization activities have largely been stupid when they were not malignant. . . . The sinister attempts of employers to identify Americanization with industrial submissiveness are with us today as in the past." A Russian priest in Cleveland expressed his feelings about the Americanization work by saying, "If I came to Russia and they made me disown everything dear to me and swear I loved hard work in the factory and bad housing I would never become a Russian." Mr. Sibray, the United States Immigration Commissioner in Pittsburgh, says, "Our Americanization Committees are largely a sham. On the average they think merely of getting the foreigner to take out citizenship and that is the last thing that ought to be done." I sent a Russian officer to make a thorough study of the Russians in Cleveland and asked him to visit the Americanization Committee because it has done notable work for many of the nationalities. In his report to me after questioning what the committee had done for the Russians, he said, "In my judgment this office exists for giving to some persons some jobs, but not getting exact

[1] *Foreign Born*, January, 1920, p. 19.

information." No doubt the Russians at the present time are very difficult to reach because of what they have suffered from the fact that the public have associated them with the Bolsheviks in Russia. The Americanization Committees are contending with the colossal problem of the alien and have naturally confined their efforts to the nationalities that responded best.

Government commissions such as the California Immigration Commission have done inestimable good in giving information to Russians and Ruthenians and forcing Americans to improve working conditions for their employees. Indeed, one of the biggest tasks in assimilation is the education of the American employer in his responsibility toward the workmen.

The American labor unions are doing a great deal toward helping to assimilate the Russians and Ruthenians. For example, the United Mine Workers of America have Russian and Ruthenian organizers and every alien member has the same privileges and benefits as do the Americans. At the meetings there are foreign speakers, and in the weekly journal there is one page printed in Slavic.

A very good type of work being carried on by Russians is that of the Russian Collegiate Institute in New York City. This work received a grant of $10,000 from the Carnegie Foundation and raised $6,000 from other sources. Its purpose is "to offer to Russian workmen within a small radius of New York City useful knowledge which will enable them to better their economic and social position."[1] All political subjects are forbidden and the school is open to all, whether pro- or anti-Bolshevik. "The institute is divided into three departments: (1) preparatory or night school, (2) academic, and

[1] From an article by Alexander Petrunkevich, the President of the Institute, in *The Standard*, February, 1920.

(3) technical. The night school prepares the workman for entrance into such institutions as Cooper Union. Instruction is given two hours every evening except Saturday and Sunday. The subjects taught are, English, Russian, geography, history, arithmetic, algebra, trigonometry, physics and chemistry." Besides the courses, the institute is carrying on lectures before larger groups than can attend the classes.

A similar school, called the Russian People's University, was started in Chicago with a foundation of $10,000, contributed by interested Russians. It also has adopted a non-political attitude. In May, 1919, it had an enrollment of about eighty. The course in agriculture proved to be the most popular, since many Russians desire to prepare for such work in Russia. Undoubtedly all this is doing much toward giving the Russian workman a fairer and better view of America. The work of the churches will be considered in another chapter.

**Use of languages.**—The figures of the Immigration Commission for 7,390 Russians [1] show that 29.5 per cent can neither read nor write, and 25.5 per cent cannot read. In the case of the Ruthenians, from 888 cases 37.4 per cent can neither read or write and 34.2 per cent cannot read. The illiteracy of Russians entering this country for the five years from 1910-1914, when the war stopped immigration, roughly averaged 35 per cent and in the case of the Ruthenians 41.2 per cent.[2] As the average Russian on entering the United States would probably claim he was literate if he could read anything at all, these figures are probably low. If then, over one-third of the Russians are illiterate, it is not strange that they do not learn English, especially when it is realized that they are practically isolated from

[1] Abstract, Vol. I, Table 77, p. 438.
[2] U. S. Bureau of Immigration Annual Reports.

Americans and they live, sleep and work together. Even so, the Russian will use American words intermingled with his Russian,—"job," "boss," "rooms," "shoes," "piecework," "pay day," "big stiff," "policeman"; profane words are even more common.

We have already mentioned the fact that in one inquiry, out of 198 literate Russians only 3 read English books and magazines. But since an average of 35 per cent are illiterate and a much larger number can read but little in their own language, how can we expect them to read English? In Mr. Cole's study in Chicago, out of 112 Russian workmen, 80 said they could speak some English, but only 12 claimed to be able to read it and in the case of these 12 no test was made. The fact is we have done little to help the Russian learn English. Even the night schools, as Professor Petrunkevich, a Russian professor at Yale University says, "although ostensibly for the benefit and instruction of uneducated and foreign workmen, are as they are at present constituted, in reality of very little help. The Russian workman has first to learn English before he can understand instruction in other subjects; but even in this, he becomes quickly discouraged. He is a stranger to the teacher who does not take into account his peculiar psychology. A few days, perhaps a few weeks of most strenuous work in the evening after the day's work at the factory, and the Russian workman gives up in despair."[1] Since these are the facts, we must make use of the Russian and Ruthenian language for lectures and for printed matter on America, if we are to have any degree of success in this gigantic task of assimilation.

**Use of racial sentiment.**—A great deal can be done by appealing to the Russian to prepare himself to return and build up his own country along the best

[1] *The Standard*, February, 1920.

lines. Whether he is a Bolshevik or an I. W. W., if he is sincere, he wants to make his native land the finest in the world. If he can be appealed to from this angle, he may later change his views and even take out citizenship papers. This has actually happened in the Protestant church work among Russians in this country.

**Learning the American mind.**—No Russian or Ruthenian can learn much of the American mind without having points of contact with Americans. As we will show in Chapter VII, for the Russian especially, these are woefully few, and often are only with the harmful elements of our life. Probably the agencies which are actually touching the foreigner such as the public schools, the social and civic organizations, the labor unions, and the religious bodies are doing what little is being done to interpret to him the America which lies underneath the huge machine that he sees.

**Naturalization.**—Perhaps the extent that Russians are learning the American mind is somewhat indicated by the number becoming naturalized citizens. The Immigration Commission in its investigation of workers in 1909 [1] found that out of 1,388 Russians, 15.1% were fully naturalized while 12.9% had first papers only. This leaves 72% who had not even taken out their first papers. The same investigation showed that out of 161 Ruthenians, 8.7% were fully naturalized and 11.2% only had their first papers, making a total of 80.1% who had not even taken out first papers. This was in 1909. Today probably even fewer of the Russians desire citizenship.

Mr. Cole in his Chicago study in 1919 found that only 4 out of 112 Russians investigated had become citizens, although three others had taken out their

[1] Abstract of Report of Immigrant Commission, Vol. I, Table 98, p. 484.

first papers. In my investigations I found many Russians who had taken out their first papers, but who openly said they would never become citizens. Indeed, over 90% of the Russians say they wish to return to Russia. They had been so persecuted by the police in the "red" raids, there has been so much vituperation wasted on the "Bolsheviks" and our press and industrial system has considered every Russian so suspicious that we cannot wonder if they look for no permanent abiding place here. We have yet to make the masses of Russians and Ruthenians desire citizenship and look upon it as an honor.

**Results as reflected by war service.**—During the war, especially after the Russian revolution, the Russians and Ruthenians gave loyal and enthusiastic support to our country. They subscribed to hundreds of thousands of Liberty Bonds, they enlisted in the army and the great majority worked in the war industries. But gradually large numbers became embittered because of their war experience. In the first place, they did not like the way in which many were forced to subscribe to war bonds. Frequently they were warned that they would be discharged if they did not subscribe; in other cases the money was simply deducted from their wages. The results are obvious. After the revolution, the Russians in France found that their brother soldiers from Russia who had been fighting with French units were held as prisoners and were refused permission to return to Russia for fear they might aid the Bolsheviks. After the armistice the Russian prisoners from Germany were similarly treated. Furthermore, the sending of United States troops including Russians into Russia to fight the Bolsheviks was distinctly unpopular. All these measures awoke in the Russian a powerful feeling of hostility and bitterness. In the place of his former patriotism there sprang up a strong resentment against America. Some of the Russians who had served a year in France came back not only to find their old jobs gone, but also to be refused others simply because they were Russians. Some were imprisoned for two months on the suspicion that they were Bolsheviks, and then were discharged for lack of evidence. Naturally many of these ex-service men began to feel that all America had wanted was to use them in dangerous fighting. But in spite of this feeling, the Russian does desire education. Out of 198 letters from Russians addressed to the Foreign Language Governmental Information Bureau, 148 wanted literature in Russian on agriculture, 138 on America, 136 on labor questions, 133 on social and political questions and 96 on general information. The following extracts from a few of their letters will show their deep longing for education: "I wanted to remain in America forever, but after the revolution I decided to go back. I do not want to go back with an empty head; if I go to Russia I want to help the Russian peasantry, and therefore while I am here I want to study scientific agriculture. I want to become what I have decided to be, namely, a man useful to humanity." "If you only can satisfy our longing to learn about America, please do it, but do it of course in the Russian language," writes a Russian from Gary, Indiana. Another from New York says, "I speak very bad English. Going to the evening school did not do me any good. In these schools seven-eighths of all the time is spent in preaching patriotism and also on getting subscriptions for the Liberty Loans. I think this is not right. A school is a place for study only." A Russian workman from Albany writes: "There is a great desire among the Russians for education. It is much needed now, for ignorance leads people to Bolshevism and Anarchism. But though there is a bureau to help the Russians in America, nothing was done to help their education in Albany, N. Y. Here the Russian colony tried to create a Union of Russian Citizens for purely educational purposes and without any political aims. But the police did not like it and did not allow it to meet for conferences and lectures."

## Chapter V

## RELIGIOUS CONDITIONS

**Old country faiths and churches retained.**—It will be remembered that the Uniat Church is made up of members of the Greek Orthodox faith who effected a compromise with Rome in 1595. The Pope was so anxious to secure their allegiance that he issued the bull, "Magnus Dominus," in that year. This permitted the Slavic liturgy, the administration of the Sacrament in both kinds to the laity, and the marriage of the clergy. The churches that accepted this compromise are called Uniat, or the United Greek Church, although they are officially named The Greek Catholic Church. The Ruthenians from Galicia are mostly Uniats, while those from Bukowina are nearly all Orthodox. They all are very religious and loyally support their churches. In many of the Pennsylvania towns one finds that the finest church in the community is the Uniat. Until the Russian revolution there was a tendency on the part of many of the Uniats to break away from the Catholic faith. The great difference between the Uniats, with their married clergy, and the Irish, Polish, German and American Catholics, with their celibate clergy, was so great that relations between them were not over cordial.

Today the Russian Orthodox Church is in financial difficulties and some Orthodox churches are going back into the Uniat fold. According to the United States Census of Religious Bodies in 1916 the Roman Catholics have 69 churches for Ruthenians with a membership of 72,393. It has been my experience in visiting Ruthenian religious services to find them very well attended. There is no doubt that great numbers of Ruthenians retain their faith in the mother church. This is not so true of scattered rural settlements where a church is not available. When, however, a great number of Ruthenians have settled, they usually secure a priest and build a church.

The Greek Orthodox Church is very much larger than the Uniat, for it includes both Russians and Ruthenians. Furthermore, until the revolution it received very substantial support from the Tsar's government. According to the 1916 Census, it had 169 churches with 99,681 members in this country. Since the revolution, the strength of the Greek Orthodox Church has considerably diminished. One of her priests in Pennsylvania told me that 90% of the Russians in America are untouched by the church, except at Christmas, Easter and on the occasions of their weddings. The growing indifference of the workmen to the church has resulted in great financial difficulty, and in some localities churches have been abandoned. In one place in Pennsylvania the priest has kept a substantial income by coöperating with the mine owners. One-half a day's wage of every Russian is deducted monthly by the company and turned over to the priest. Unfortunately, most of the priests have found that the companies have turned a deaf ear to their appeals for help. Even in the case of the priest mentioned above, he has to pay a heavy rent for the use of company land for his school building, and the customary discount on the price of coal granted to the mine workers is not extended to the church.

The deeply religious nature of the Russian people has been aptly expressed by Stephen Graham: "The Russians are always en route for some place where they may find out something about God." In Russia they are continually crossing themselves and repeating "Guspody Pomiluy"—"Lord be merciful"; but here in America they gradually forget some of the outward forms. Nevertheless, one can see even in their everyday speech a sympathy for the unfortunate and a forgiving spirit which is of the essence of religion. For example, if a man is arrested he is not called wicked but "neschastny" or unlucky. One of their common expressions at parting is "proschai," or forgive. A few of their proverbs will further illustrate this depth of religious feeling:

"God who gave us teeth, he will also give us the bread."
"God gave us the body, he will also give us health."
"Where there is love, there is also God."
"Who riseth early, to him God gives."
"The church is not built of logs, but of (human) ribs."
"The evil man is like charcoal, if he does not burn you he blackens you."

Religious feeling where ignorance is also present inevitably takes on superstitious practices, and we could not expect that the masses of Russian people who have been so shut out from all enlightenment would be any exception to the rule. But even the superstitions show a deep sense of the presence of God in life. A friend of mine in Russia once noticed that the people try to stop the spread of fire by placing the ikon, or religious picture, between the fire and the next house. And when they leave the old homes to journey into a far country, they bring with them these same sacred ikons. In America nearly every room has its sacred ikon and most of the Russians still continue to wear baptismal crosses. Two Russians who had taken an active part in the steel strike and had only hard words for the church, still believe in God and venerate those things which stand for Him to them and had the ikon of Christ with the wreath of thorns in a corner of their room. A Russian Orthodox priest in Brooklyn told me that 75% of the Russian workmen are opposed to the church, although they believe in God. Indeed, one of the outstanding facts regarding the Russian workmen is that while they are skeptical about the church they still worship in their hearts the divine personality, which, they feel, the church does not honestly represent and serve.

The second generation of Russians and Ruthenians tend even more to forsake their old-country faith. In the first place, they speak and read English much better than Russian. Still less do many of them understand the Slavic services. The result is that while the more religious parents take their children to the church, as the children grow older they tend to be less and less attracted by it. Several of the Greek Orthodox priests admitted to me that they could not hold the second generation and that if they are to keep the native-born Russians, they will have to conduct their services in English.

**Forms of religious break-up.**—The Greek Orthodox Church is not so organized as readily to adapt itself to change. Indeed, its greatest boast is that it has never changed the doctrines of the universal church as established by the ecumenical councils. It attacks both Protestantism and Roman Catholicism on the ground that they continually change to meet new and temporary needs. In a letter of the Russian Bishop Nicholas, head of the Orthodox Mission to Japan, this is clearly brought out: "It is the Orthodox Church alone which can give to drink from the fount of the sweetness of the word of God, to those who come to her for she *alone* has *preserved* the divine doctrine just as it was committed to her, and will preserve it unchanged to the end of the ages, without adding to or taking from it a single iota."[1]

As a result of this principle, the Orthodox Church has a tendency to prove unadaptable to American conditions and, as a whole, the church in America follows exactly the leadership of the church in Russia. Consequently, although it is so sorely needed, they are doing but little social service work. The Russian workman is now in a new world with a thousand new ideas thrust in upon him daily. He is meeting those who scoff at religion and is constantly being exploited. He needs social help and legal and medical aid, but his church does not adequately meet this need of Christianity applied to a changing social order. As soon as the Bolsheviks took the power, the priests strove by sermon and pen to attack them. One Russian priest in Cleveland handed out circulars urging his parishioners to volunteer to fight against the Bolsheviks. This again antagonized the Russian workmen. They suspected that this policy was pursued only because the Bolsheviks were socialistic and had separated the church from the state.

As a consequence of this general attitude, some of the Russian workmen became atheists. They are always careful, however, to say that while they do not believe in God they do believe in the religion of humanity. They believe, so they claim, in serving the mass of the workmen,—that is their religion. Still others, and much the larger proportion, are free thinkers. They have faith in God, but not in the church as constituted today. Many of them believe that war is opposed to the teachings of Christ —the writings of Tolstoy have influenced large num-

[1] The italics are mine.

bers in this. Among the second generation of Russians, especially, I found many who seemed to be drifting, without really substituting anything in the place of the church. These people are waiting for a strong, virile religion, whose first approach shall be through ministering to the needs of every day.

#### FORMS OF RELIGIOUS REALIGNMENTS

**Schismatics and sectarians.**—It is estimated that in Russia there are between fifteen and twenty million sectarians. The great schism from the Orthodox Church took place in the middle of the sixteenth century. The General Council of the Church in 1666 excommunicated all who refused to accept the revised liturgy and those who were thus excommunicated became known as the Old Believers. They soon split into those who had no priests—"priestless"—and those who had. The former organized a lay leadership.

Besides this chief sect, many other fanatical ones sprang up. There were the sects of "Wanderers," of "Molchalniki" or mutes, who believed in being silent; the sect of "Non-prayers," who opposed praying; the Jumpers, who worked themselves into an ecstasy, some of whom became licentious and some were ascetics; the sect of "Skoptzy" or Eunuchs, who believed in castration and held that the second coming of Christ would take place when their membership reached the mystic number of 144,000. Besides these, there were the "Dukhobory" or "Wrestlers of the Spirit." They refuse to acknowledge the authority of the Bible and believe in the living conscience within the hearts of men. They are vegetarians, pacifists and communists. Another sect, the "Molokans," or milk drinkers, have a strong following in Russia. They are probably so named because they drink milk on fast days.

During the reign of Catherine II, German colonists settled in South Russia. They were Baptists, Mennonites, and pietistic Evangelicals. Soon many of the Russians embraced the Baptist faith. They were called Stundists after the German *Stunde*, for they held services for about an hour in length. After the revolution of 1905 foreign missionaries were permitted to work in Russia. The Baptists secured the largest number of converts; their present membership exceeds 29,000 with 178 churches, 472 meeting places, 349 Sunday schools and a theological seminary. The Methodists have 8 churches and 6 preachers with about 700 members.

The persecutions which many of these sects met in Russia were the cause of the members' emigrating to the United States. In North Dakota there are today about 10,000 Stundists. When these Russian Baptists first reached North Dakota they were very poor and had to borrow enough for a start from the loan companies at heavy rates of interest. The first year proved disastrous, as the crops were a failure. The Russians were penniless and without food. A friendly American placed an advertisement in the Minneapolis papers asking for help for these starving Russians and in a short time several wagon loads of flour, coal, shoes and all kinds of canned goods were sent to the Russians, who have never forgotten. They have become American citizens, and believe in America largely because of this friendly act.

Through the influence of Count Tolstoy and others, many of the Dukhobors were helped to emigrate to Canada. After they had made a success there, they were visited by some of the Russian Molokans. The latter did not find Canada inviting, but after travelling along the Pacific Coast were favorably impressed with Los Angeles. Beginning in 1905, they began to emigrate to Los Angeles and con-

tinued to do so up to the outbreak of the World War.
At the present time there are in Los Angeles about
4,500 Molokans or milk-drinkers, 50 Dukhobors and
400 Subotniks or Judaized Russians. The Molokans,
in turn, are split into 3,100 Priguni or "Jumpers,"
and 200 Postoyani or "Steadfast ones." The great
majority of these now want to return to Russia to
enjoy the new freedom which they believe has been
won there. There have also been several communist and coöperative experiments in America which
have not proved successful. In Harrison, Tenn., a
colony of anarchists started a commune in 1913,
but it failed within a year. Others have been started
in California, Minnesota, Texas, and New York, but
most of them with similar results.

Besides these sectarian movements in the United
States, there has been a split in the Russian Orthodox Church in America. Until the revolution, the
Tsar's government, through the Holy Synod,
granted about $40,000 yearly for the work of the
Orthodox Church in America. After the revolution
the church in Russia was separated from the state
and no money was sent to America. This close relationship between the Tsar's government and the
church in America naturally made for an autocratic
management. All the titles to the property throughout the United States were supposed to belong to
the bishop of the Greek Orthodox Church in
America. The Russian workmen, who had given
the money to buy the land and buildings, slowly becoming imbued with American ideals, demanded a
greater measure of control over the property which
they felt they had paid for. Besides the influence
of American traditions, the revolution in Russia has
powerfully stimulated this feeling. The desire for
a more democratic control caused conflicts in many
churches in America. For example, it has been reported that in Chicago the workmen who had paid

their savings for church expenses demanded an accounting. At last they became so insistent that the priest preached them a sermon on the text, "Let not thy left hand know what thy right hand doeth," stating that the gifts were given to God and needed no accounting. This so enraged some of the workmen that they broke up the service, upon which the priest used his heavy gilt cross as a club on the heads of his dissatisfied parishioners. The fight ended in a split among the members and the starting of an "Independent" church. This church used many of the old ritual forms, but the title to the property rested with the parishioners.

This democratic movement has spread rapidly until now there are independent churches in Chicago, Detroit, New York, Boston, Philadelphia, Brooklyn, Baltimore, Bayonne City, N. J., and Lawrence, Mass. Ordinarily these churches carry on a larger educational and social work than do the Orthodox ones. The increase in the difficulties of the Russian Orthodox Church is indicated by the fact that since the revolution the acting Bishop has had fifteen law suits on his hands, five of which were to secure the control of church property. This independent movement and the growing estrangement of the Russian from his church, while discouraging from an Orthodox point of view, is nevertheless an indication of the growing democratic spirit of the Russians.

Of course the great majority of Russian priests remain Orthodox and many of them are doing a splendid work for their parishioners. They are sharing the isolation of the mining camps at meager salaries and are giving their countrymen the inspiration which comes from beautiful religious services and sacraments.

**Protestant church affiliation.**—The large number of Russian sects in America has tended to increase the number of converts in the Protestant churches.

Very much more work has been done among them than among the Ruthenians. The United States Census of Religious Bodies in 1916 gave the following data on Protestant Russian Churches: The Baptists—4 Russian churches with a total of 174 members and 4 mixed churches with a total of 1,350 members; The Disciples of Christ—4 Russian churches with 194 members; The Seventh Day Adventists—4 Russian churches with 171 members and 1 mixed church with 26 enrolled; The Methodist Episcopal Church—1 Russian church with 200 members and 1 mixed church of 350 members; The Presbyterians—1 Russian church of 25 members and 2 mixed churches with 1,015 members; The Mennonites—1 Russian church of 47 members; The Protestant Episcopal—1 mixed church with 1,071 members; The Church of Christ—1 mixed church with 135 members. The Roman Catholic churches numbered 122, with 124,285 members, and the Eastern Orthodox, 168, with 99,406 members. At the present time (1921) I believe there are 31 meeting places for Russian Baptists alone, which shows the progress the Protestant work has been making since 1916.

When we turn to the same statistics in regard to the Ruthenians we find: The Presbyterian church—2 Ruthenian churches with 779 members, 2 mixed churches with 1,698 members; The Protestant Episcopal Church with 1 mixed church of 65 members; The Baptists with 1 mixed church with 45 members. The Roman Catholics had 70 churches and 74,860 members.[1] In the case of the Ruthenian churches it would have been possible to have increased the number of Protestant churches to six had every mixed church been included.[2]

Undoubtedly big gains in Protestant affiliation are to be made in the years just ahead. The ground

[1] U. S. Census of Religious Bodies, 1916.
[2] Many of above figures include adherents.

work has been laid and if the Protestant Church is awake to her opportunity, growth will be rapid. Probably the Baptist Church, both in America and Russia, has done more than any other Protestant denomination among the Russians.

A brief historical statement of the growth of their work in New York City by Dr. Sears is of interest as showing that it was a schism in the Baptist work which resulted in the founding of the Disciple Mission among the Russians and that the Baptists have been responsible for the origin of at least one other denominational group.

### FORMS OF RELIGIOUS APPROACH

**Social settlement.**—There is, so far as I know, no social settlement ministering exclusively to the Russians and Ruthenians. There are a number that include these among other nationalities, but most of them have not had a paid worker speaking these languages and hence have had to confine their efforts very largely to the children who speak English. The social settlement is doing a splendid work in bringing the Russian and Ruthenian into contact with American ideals and with friendly American citizens, but it seldom does a distinctively religious work. It is true that some of them are run by religious denominations such as, for instance, the settlement of the Baptist City Mission in Philadelphia or that of the Episcopal City Mission in New York, and others like the Settlement run by Union Theological Seminary are inter-denominational. Unfortunately settlement work has not yet to any degree acted as a channel into church membership for Russians and Ruthenians.

**The institutional church.** — The institutional church is probably the best means of reaching the Russians and Ruthenians. The Rev. George G. Hollingshead of the St. Paul's Methodist Episcopal Church in Jersey City, N. J., has done splendid work among the Russians through this means. He began by simply throwing open a large room for their meetings to a group of Russians, allowing them to organize in their own way and to hold meetings as they wished. They called themselves "The Russian Self-Educated Circle." Soon the number of members reached about sixty. They had an open forum every Saturday night following a lecture, and classes in English were held on Monday and Tuesday nights. Later mathematics and civics were added. Voluntarily this group began to make contributions to the church expenses and finally several of them joined the church on their own initiative. They said they wanted to support a church which permitted Russians to meet in it and conduct meetings in their own way. The Church of All Nations in New York City has been doing valuable work with the Russians as well as with the other nationalities. The Labor Temple, in New York City, has also been conducting an open forum on social, civic, economic, political and religious subjects. These have attracted some Russians, but there has been no distinctly religious work among them. The Gary Chapel and Neighborhood House in Gary, Ind., has done notable work in helping all the various nationalities. Eight national foreign societies hold meetings in the house. There were classes in English, boy scout work and religious services. The institutional church can be made a powerful instrument in reaching Russians and Ruthenians, but it must be located in the neighborhood in which they live and eventually must have workers on its staff who speak their languages.

**Evangelism.**—The preaching of personal loyalty to Jesus Christ should always be the primary message of the church to the Russian and Ruthenian.

Religious teaching and the evangelistic method must be a part of every church work for foreigners. Music from the Salvation Army reaching the Russians on the street has successfully been used by the Russian Baptist minister in Buffalo; others have found that few Russians or Ruthenians have been touched in this way. Undoubtedly if a Russian has a talent for street preaching he can reach his countrymen in this way. But by far the greater number of the churches working among the Russians find that evangelistic meetings are more effective. In order to bring permanent results in church membership and church life, they must be closely tied up to a service program which will meet the needs all around the circle of a man's living. When this is done and when we lay less stress upon the points of difference between denominational creeds, there will be less of a tendency to fanaticism among those who naturally might be so inclined. One Orthodox Russian priest in California has said that 80% of the poorer classes of Russians in that state belong to fanatical sects, as the "Molokans," Holy Rollers, Holy Jumpers, Anti-Baptists, and Anti-Priest believers.

Equipment is naturally a big problem. Frequently, as in Pittsburgh among a population of thousands of Russians and Ruthenians, there is only a small rented store room to meet their religious needs. It is doubtless inevitable that the work should begin in a small way before it can grow larger, but it does seem unfortunate that the immigrant who is so impressed with our huge buildings and industrial establishments should not find a larger and more complete plant awaiting his religious needs. The institutional church, for this reason alone, has a greater advantage.

**By a minister of kin.**—The men who are today doing the most effective evangelistic work among the Russians in the United States are Russians. Undoubtedly the big handicap of the Russian language is one reason for this. Another is that those Americans who do understand Russian are usually drawn to other fields. Either they go to Russia or they become engaged in social, civic or commercial work. The Russian ministers have an advantage in knowing better the psychology of the Russian immigrant and furthermore, can speak the language perfectly. Too often they lack education. Nearly all the students in the Baptist Seminary in New Jersey, for example, had not been in high school and many of them had not even finished the grammar school. The reason for this is that the majority of converts are from the peasant class who have emigrated to America.

### LITERATURE

**The secular press.**—The Russian secular press is almost entirely in the hands of Jews, and hence is more or less antagonistic to the Protestant and Greek Orthodox churches. The Ukrainian secular press, on the other hand, in the case of several newspapers, is working in close touch with the church, which is Roman Catholic. It cannot, therefore, be very open-minded toward Protestant church work.

**The religious press.**—The religious press keeps changing frequently as new sects spring up and established publications die out. A list of the more important religious periodicals appearing in the Russian and Ukrainian languages is found in Appendix C. Of the Russian papers, five are issued monthly, and only two more often than once a week. Many of these periodicals may be doing much good, but are unattractive in form and more or less fanatical. Their tone is indicated by verse such as "The Blood of the Son" which appeared in 1920. This may appeal to a few but certainly would not touch the majority of Russian readers. The material in most of these periodicals seems to be theological and unconnected with the conditions of daily living. The *Norodny Poychenia* is the Russelite magazine and anyone who is familiar with the literature of that sect knows the kind of articles which they circulate depicting the end of the world as now impending.

The truth is that there is not a single paper for the thousands of Russians or Ruthenians in this country which can compare with our Protestant English religious weeklies. It is to be regretted that those denominations who could get together, cannot unite in publishing a first class interdenominational religious paper. It should combine comments on news items, stories, a children's page, educational features, as well as religious instruction and inspiration.

**Tracts.**—I have read over fifty tracts printed in Russian and find that in general they take for granted the literal word-for-word divine inspiration of the Bible. They use the proof text method. Quite a considerable number are too controversial to be really effective. Many of them are not adapted to the Russian Slav because they are not based upon Russian psychology. On the other hand the pamphlets attacking belief in God as a superstition, put out by the Union of Russian Workers, are really far more effective for their destructive purpose. For example, one of them published in 1918, *The Fact of God*, attempts to show in a clever scientific way that (1) the hypothesis of God is unnecessary, (2) that it is not useful, (3) that it is nonsense, (4) that it is criminal. Dogmatic tracts cannot meet such arguments; they must be met with reason and love. In order to do this, the tracts must deal with subjects with which the Russians are familiar in their everyday experience. This should include the bad boss and the good foreman, the hard grind of factory life and the crowded conditions in the tenement. The illustrated story form of presentation is especially desirable for the average Russian.

One set of tracts should be developed for the bulk of Russian laborers who constitute ninety-five per cent of the Russians in this country. There should be another set for the intelligent Christians and for their ministers and leaders. The tracts and booklets examined were printed by eight different religious organizations. It is very difficult to classify the tracts because they might fall under any one of several headings. I believe ten might be considered devotional, fourteen theological, eleven evangelical and two sociological. There were sixteen story pamphlets, but three of these were included under one of the other headings. Of the fifty, thirty-six might be considered positive, and fourteen controversial or negative. Twenty-one were translations from the English, and twenty-five seemed to be written for the Russians. The four gospels were not included in this last summary.

The size and paper used for the tracts were suitable but in some cases a larger type would have been better. More illustrations could have been used giving greater value for the ordinary Russian. Most of them were written in simple everyday language.

It was interesting—and disappointing—to note that the majority of the tracts expressed the thought of twenty-five or thirty years ago. They did not have the modern social viewpoint. For example, a tract by Mr. Bokmelder, a teacher in the International Baptist Seminary at East Orange, N. J., on *The Anti-Christ* appears to be attacking the labor unions and is so considered even by religious Russian workmen whom I consulted. It says, "We soon are nearing the time when all unions will unite in one union at the head of which will be the Anti-Christ or beast. At the present time the Unions give their members membership cards, but in the Kingdom of the Anti-Christ all citizens of his must have the name of the beast on their forehead." The Russians, since the revolution, are particularly susceptible to the social gospel, yet there was only one booklet which could really be considered as written from this point of view. This was Rauschenbusch's *Social Teachings of Jesus* translated by the Y. M. C. A. The few biographical references in the tracts mentioned no Russian names—which would have been the more effective—but American leaders. Most of them presupposed too great a knowledge of the Bible for the ordinary Russian, although this was not true of the stories. None of the tracts seemed especially adapted for the group in America as contrasted with those in the home land. Some were printed in Petrograd and are evidently used interchangeably here and in Russia.

The gospels in illustrated pamphlet form are very valuable, as are extracts from the Old and New Testaments; perhaps some slight comment to accompany them would make them still more useful.

Devotional booklets of the type of Fosdick's *Manhood of the Master,* and *The Meaning of Prayer,* which have been translated and published by the Y. M. C. A., are excellent for Russian students, and for those who have been educated. For the Russian workmen still more simple books should be developed. Theological pamphlets should, undoubtedly, be written in popular and simple language, and should deal with the fundamental points of our Christian faith.

Disputed matters between the different denominations should be avoided as far as possible. Probably the greatest need of all is for pamphlets which deal with social questions. These should take up the life problems of the Russians in America. They should make the position of the church absolutely clear regarding social justice in industry and commerce, and should make the Russian feel that where he has been exploited, the church stands with him against his oppressor.

The Russians do not realize the dangers from tuberculosis and other diseases, and know little of proper precautionary measures and personal hygiene. Besides pamphlets on these subjects there should be others which tell the notable achievements of the great Russian leaders, of the truly wonderful religious men which Russia has produced. Extracts from many of the lay Russian writers could certainly be used to great advantage.

General literature.—Very little of American literature has been translated into Russian. The Y. M. C. A. has probably done more than has any other agency. They have had books translated and printed on technical and vocational subjects such as farming; on popular science such as Roubakine's *What is in the Heavens?*; on health such as Exner's *The Rational Sex Life for Men;* on biography such as Booker T. Washington's *Up From Slavery*. They also have books on history, and school books for boys and girls. The Russian Division of the Foreign Language Governmental Information Service Bureau has also translated an American history and other books. There still remains much that can be done along this line to teach the Russian and Ruthenian American ideals and the American mind.

To love our Russian and Ruthenian neighbors as ourselves is the injunction. The Russians and Ruthenians are longing for a friendly American hand and we have extended it to but a few on the fringe. We have but to lift our eyes and look upon fields already white unto a harvest more rich than we have dreamed. But the laborers indeed are few.

## Chapter VI

## SPECIAL RELIGIOUS PROBLEMS

### LEADERSHIP OF FOREIGN LANGUAGE CHURCHES

Bolsheviks or Brothers? They can be regarded as a red menace, a bogey or an obligation, according to one's viewpoint. On page 65 is a photograph of a poster found in the "House of the Masses" in Detroit, appealing to Russians to help their brothers who have been arrested. Essentially, this is a religious appeal since it asks help for those in distress. Yet there are many of us who at first would condemn them for such activity. Instead of condemnation they need friendliness and help. What a contribution to church life would their Russian traits be—their depth of religious feeling, love of music, generous sympathy, group loyalty, their willingness to suffer for an ideal. It is here that foreign language churches must assume leadership.

**Kinsmen trained in their native land.**—In Russia and Galicia there are not at the present time, adequate theological seminaries aside from the Greek Orthodox and the Catholic. Nevertheless, there may be exceptional Russians and Ruthenians coming to this country, who have already had university or theological training. They should be given the best, in further preparation, that America can offer. Mr. Fetler is one example; he came from Russia and for a time was associated with the Baptist work in New York City and later on was head of the Russian Bible and Educational Institute in Philadelphia which has an enrollment of 120 Russians and Ukrainians. There are some Russian Orthodox priests who have had training in Russia, who are sincere and earnest men. Dr. Hecker, a Russian Methodist minister, formerly at the head of the Church of All Nations in New York City, says that for real coöperation he would one hundred times rather work with the Orthodox priests than with sectarian-minded Protestant preachers. Much could be done to help these priests bring the message of Christ more effectively to their Russian brothers. They need stereopticon slides for talks, books in Russian for sermon material, and instruction and help in American church methods. The friendly spirit which they showed to me on my visits and their oft-expressed desire to know more Americans, leads me to believe that coöperation with them would be more than possible.

**Kinsmen trained in America.**—Most of the native Russian and Ruthenian workers in this country have been trained here. They can reach the hearts of their fellow-countrymen as almost no one else can. The American has the barrier of a foreign language to overcome, and usually has not had sufficient experience of the kind the foreigner has undergone to appreciate his feelings. On the other hand, the Christian Russian or Ruthenian with a passion to present God's truth to his fellow-countrymen understands life from their angle. Very likely he himself has been through much of it. Usually these foreign leaders are recruited from men whose religious life has been awakened and deepened after coming to America. Training is then the problem. In our own colleges and seminaries they can grow to understand the American point of view and know how to present the best of our ideals. Even the Russian Orthodox Church has found the need of having her own training school for priests in this country and now maintains two of them.

One difficulty for the Russians and Ruthenians who have been trained in America is that they are doing a mission and pioneer work. Consequently they are not paid the salaries which their training would naturally call for. I have talked with several Protestant Russian pastors who declared that they could no longer endure struggling on at the meager pittance given them by their denominational boards. They said they would prefer to work as laborers in a factory. Of course we must make sure that the foreign leaders are consecrated men who are willing to sacrifice for their work, but it is unfortunate, to say the least, to make the Russian or Ruthenian feel that he is inferior to the American worker.

Another difficulty with American-trained Russians is that it is easy to get out of sympathy with their fellow countrymen who are working in factory and mine. The workers in one town in Ohio told a Russian social investigator, "The clergy are very far from the workers and cannot understand our life and need. They cannot help us in a practical way. They are existing not for us but for themselves." Undoubtedly it would be excellent training for such leaders—and perhaps not Russians only —were they required to work during the summer as laborers in the factories and mines in which their kinsmen toil. This would give them a sympathy and understanding for their brothers that nothing else could. A religious leader, himself a foreigner and working for all the nationalities in Youngstown, Ohio, wrote, "The training of Russian leaders should enable them to explain to these people natural science correctly, not the way it has been preached by Bakunin and others. They are all permeated with some of these theories. They should have a broad and practical religious education, not the old passive kind that has brought them to ruin." A Russian Protestant preacher said regarding the kind of leaders needed, "College men who specialize in sociology and economics in order that they may be leaders in interpreting the social and economic problems of the immigrant as well as his religious ones."

In fact, until the Russian preachers know from observation that most of the foreigners never see the real America, that they are too often exploited by other foreigners and by Americans, they cannot have that sympathy for them which alone will reach the heart. As a Ruthenian priest has well stated, "My people do not live in America. They live underneath America. America goes on over their heads."[1] Every alien church leader must be close to the experiences of his people. A Russian Protestant preacher for example who is bitterly hostile to the Bolsheviks must understand and tactfully deal with Russian workmen who believe in Soviet Russia or he cannot reach the masses of his countrymen in America. Sympathy, love, understanding and reverence for the personality of every humble Russian is the only key to unlock their hearts.

**Americans trained in foreign lands.**—It is naturally easy to accept foreign-born leadership for the Russians and Ruthenians. In our anxiety to extend the work, however, we must realize that American leadership is imperative. The Russian or Ruthenian pastor, be he ever so successful, can never command the respect and confidence of the American church leaders that an American will. Furthermore, the Russians are always suspicious of one from their own number, paid by someone else, who is preaching to them. They do not have quite the same feeling toward an American. They are rather surprised that when he could secure so much larger remuneration in other lines he will come to help them. For instance, a year ago the writer was vis-

[1] H. B. Grose, *Aliens or Americans.*

iting in Lawrence, Massachusetts. Being interested in the Russians he attended their church, found that they were without a pastor and that the workmen were running the church independently. These plain Russians then called a meeting at which the American spoke and afterwards the workmen showered him with thanks. They even wanted to know if he couldn't help them secure a pastor. Yet these same Russians were considered as Bolsheviks, anarchists and I. W. W.'s by the local press during the strike.

The immigrant should first be met by a Christian worker from among his own countrymen, speaking his language, understanding his viewpoint. Afterwards the American who has the right vision can do more than the Russian leader in bringing the Russian and Ruthenian in touch with our ideals and institutions. Furthermore, the American can do what is almost equally needed, if not more so, interpret the Russian and Ruthenian to Americans. His task would not only be to help the foreigner assimilate the best of America, but to make America assimilate the best that is in the Russian and Ruthenian. He would aid in preventing the exploitation of the alien and in giving to the foreigner the square deal in industry. As Shriver in his *Immigrant Forces* has stated, "The immigrant and industrial communities of this country offer unparalleled opportunities for service to young men of heroic consecration, men with a grasp upon the significance of American democracy and American institutions, trained in modern scientific methods, in sociology and philanthropy, and with a sympathetic acquaintance with the life, language, history, and religious traditions of the immigrants."

In order really to help him here, the background out of which he has come should be seen and studied by the American leader. He must live with the native Russians, see their home life, and understand their ideals and language. It is small wonder that the most successful American workers among foreigners have had some training in their home lands. Men like the Rev. Joel B. Hayden of Cleveland, the Rev. Kenneth D. Miller and Harvey Anderson of New York City have all had this privilege. It is an indispensable prerequisite for the largest work among Russians and Ruthenians in America.

**Work of men and women.**—There has been very little work done for the Russians by women. Some church work has been carried on, the Y. W. C. A. has made some progress, and a few settlement houses have used Russian workers. There is no question but that sincere and consecrated women workers can do much that men cannot do. They can go into the tenement homes and reach the women and children as no man can. In matters of cooking, the care and feeding of children, and in home nursing they have an approach to the home of the immigrant which eventually may lead into the church. The road to the heart of the foreigner often lies through his children and many a beginning has been made through Sunday schools and kindergartens organized by women.

Miss Jones at the Methodist Temple in Philadelphia is an illustration of one who has been doing evangelistic work. There are now almost two hundred attending these meetings and many have been converted. Other women have been able to reach the men also through English classes. On the other hand a woman worker cannot take as active an interest in the labor of the foreigner in factory and mine as a man can. He is able to go anywhere at any time in our crowded foreign sections; a woman cannot move so freely. Furthermore there is still something in the mores of the Russians and Ruthenians which makes them accept a man for a minis-

## SPECIAL RELIGIOUS PROBLEMS

ter more quickly than they would a woman. It has been their experience in the past that only men have been priests. Nevertheless there is no clear dividing line between the work of men and women. Both are needed and both can be effective if they know the social, the economic and the religious needs of the people, sympathize with and love them and give themselves unreservedly in self-sacrificing service.

### FOREIGN LANGUAGE TRAINING SCHOOLS

**Denominational.**—In talking with Russian Protestant pastors, both those who had been trained in colleges and seminaries and those who had not, I found them all agreed that the best method of training foreign leaders is to have them go through our American colleges and seminaries and mingle with American men. Shriver in his *Immigrant Forces* quotes a resolution adopted by American and Magyar pastors which might well apply to the Russian and Ruthenian work: "We do not believe in a double standard of education or qualification for the ministry, one for foreign-speaking men and a second for English-speaking men. We believe both standards should be high and that our foreign-speaking candidates should apply themselves with the same devotion and painstaking in preparation for the ministry as is expected of all candidates in the church."

When we come to work out the practical side of this plan, however, we find that many of the men who desire to enter these fields of Christian work are too old to take all the preparation necessary for entrance to our American theological seminaries. Many of them do not even know English. To meet this situation, a number of our denominations have organized schools which conduct classes in the Russian language. Thus the Baptists maintained in

1920 a Russian Baptist Bible Institute in New York City which trained religious leaders in the Russian language. The great difficulty here, as one of the students explained to me, was that the Russian students are isolated and so do not mix with any Americans. As they all speak Russian and have little need for the English, here again they are living in a world apart from American life. This school has now (1921) become a branch of an International Seminary at East Orange, N. J.

A number of our American theological seminaries maintain Slavic departments, having the advantage of being closely affiliated with the American. Students who know enough English can take work along with the Americans. Such a school is the Baldwin Wallace Theological Seminary at Berea, Ohio. A list of various theological seminaries and schools which receive Russian or Ruthenian students is included in Appendix B.

**Interdenominational.**—It is natural, since our Protestant churches are only in the first stages of federation, that the denominational school should be the first to meet these needs of the foreigner. As far as I have been able to learn, there is no real interdenominational foreign language training school in America although we use this plan on the foreign field. We have our American interdenominational seminaries such as Union Theological in New York City, but there are no Russians or Ruthenians in attendance. Wherever it is possible to do so, the Russians and Ruthenians should certainly go to such a seminary with its splendid Christian teachers. They would then come to know a little of the best in America. Still, for those Russians who are inadequately prepared, the Christian forces of America should provide an interdenominational school. One of the Protestant Russian pastors expressed to me his deep feeling that our failure to do more among the Russians is due to interdenominational jealousies and rivalries. At present one denomination in a city will compete with another for Russian attendance. One minister will condemn as false the doctrines of the other Protestant church. This leads to the state of mind of one Russian worker, "All churches disagree on what they believe, one says the other bad, we don't believe any, they all are working for money too, we only believe in God and try to live good lives." Even a Russian Baptist minister in Pennsylvania said, "In the churches of New York among the Russians there are Presbyterians, Methodists, Baptists, Pentecostals, Disciples, Mennonites. The Russian people go from one to the other and say they are all crazy. They preach only denominationalism, they do not preach the gospel. The Russian people believe that the real religion is wanting to do good and serve God, and have no interest in our American denominationalism."

An interdenominational seminary for Russians would lead all the students to see that the different churches are coöperating forces for bringing in the Kingdom of God. They would realize that the church is one, although it has different forms of expression. It is true that all the denominations would be unwilling to join in such an undertaking, but this should not deter those who can unite from being the pioneers in this eminently Christian union.

**Polyglot training schools.**—Polyglot training schools are good in that they draw together the different nationalities, but do not as a rule have sufficient Americanizing influences at work. The Russians and Ruthenians need the contact with Americans. If such a foreign language training school offers classes in English, the students should eventually be able to take a year of special training in an American seminary. If most of their subjects are given in the various foreign languages, the students do not get much benefit from their intercourse with other nationalities. Too often they see the weaknesses and failures of certain groups, not their virtues, thus making unchristian racial antagonisms possible. On the other hand, there are experiences which all the foreigners have in common. They have come as immigrants to a foreign land. They are more or less unacquainted with the real America. Most of the different nationalities labor in the relatively harder lines of industrial work, live in the congested districts of our larger cities and are thrown in touch with each other in their life in factory and tenement. Consequently, all have common problems which can be shared and which can be dealt with in such detail as would not be possible in an American seminary. The polyglot seminary may at present be necessary from a practical standpoint but the interdenominational school in which the foreigner mingles with the American would certainly prove more effective.

**Americanizing influences.**—Whether the foreign training school is denominational, interdenominational, or polyglot the biggest problem of all is to be sure that the Americanizing influences are adequate. Usually such seminaries have courses in the English language and lectures on American customs and ideals. While this is necessary it is not enough. The Russian and Ruthenian must be brought into contact with American life. One excellent method is to have observation courses where the foreign students are taken to the various American institutions such as our courts, our schools, our settlements, our prisons, our churches and our factories; they are then required to write their criticisms. This opens the way for class room discussion on just what are the ideals of America. The foreign students ought also to mingle with American theological students, make friends with them, and come into their home life. Where this is impossible an arrangement should be made whereby each student could work with some one American.

Further, if the Russian or Ruthenian students are capable of doing so, they should be sent out to speak before American churches and Sunday Schools. This helps them to see our best American life and helps the American people to be sympathetic with the foreigner.

One of the best means of helping our Russian and Ruthenian brothers in America is by assisting wherever possible the Orthodox Russian and Ruthenian leaders. The Christian forces of America have not yet done what they can to help the Russian Greek Orthodox priests. Many of these men are longing for help. Several of them have asked me to refer them to American agencies that could furnish stereopticon slides which they could use. In the task of coöperating with these foreign church leaders already scattered broadcast over America, much can be done. Few of these men have yet been Americanized. One of them expressed to me the opinion that all the churches of America are sold to money; they do not dare speak openly for the rights of the workers, and in strike situations they side with the capitalist. "They have betrayed their Christ for a mess of pottage. They are sold to the devil." Surely if our Christian forces should not only try to Americanize the Protestant Russian students, but the Russian priests as well, they would multiply their effectiveness.

## Chapter VII

## RELATIONS WITH THE AMERICAN PEOPLE

**First impressions.**—The majority of Russians and Ruthenians are almost as completely isolated from the American people as if they were in the heart of giant Russia. They have no points of contact with the sound elements of American life. The dream of the Russian as he leaves his native shore is that everything is beautiful in America. It is the land of liberty and equality but he begins to feel that perhaps he has been hoodwinked almost as soon as he reaches Ellis Island. The Russians claim that the coarse and brutal treatment they receive at the immigrant stations is far worse than that in the Russia of the Tsars. Certainly the wholesale tagging of the immigrant, the physical inspection, the turning back of the eyelids, rushed through with machine-like regularity resembles more the inspection of cattle than of thousands of human souls. Only this year Commissioner Wallis, head of the immigrant station at Ellis Island, has complained of the methods of his subordinates who seem to think that an immigrant's time is worth nothing at all. It is small wonder that their first taste of liberty does not appeal. Then as they push on to their destination at Gary, or Pittsburgh, or Chicago, there is no one who tries to help them. I remember meeting two Russians at the Grand Central Station in New York. They were wandering about trying to find out when their train would go. Their inquiries in broken English met no response from the busy ticket agent. They stood beside their bags and baggage, a little picture of Russia in New York. They would ask passers-by about the train but at no time did anyone stop more than to say, "We don't know." One richly dressed woman replied as she would to a dog, "Get away from me." The look on their faces when I helped them showed how deep their perplexity and apprehension had been.

Indeed, the treatment at Ellis Island and in the railroad trains frequently awakens other sentiments than love for the new home. The immigrant has to learn at once the dangers of exploitation which await him. If he goes into the railroad dining room he is usually hustled out. If he follows the advice of a seemingly kind friend as to where to eat he is often robbed of his money. Sometimes his baggage is stolen, and there have even been cases of the abduction of his daughter or wife before he has been on American soil twelve hours. At best, the first impressions of America are discouraging because the treatment of a vast throng of incoming strangers has not yet been put on a friendly enough basis. We still are doing largely only the things that will safeguard America from undesirables and not enough genuinely to help the foreigner.

**Real Americanization.**—Real Americanization is a spiritual thing. It means that the Russian or Ruthenian loves our country and is willing to sacrifice in its behalf. This love can be created only by his experiencing that which is worthy of loyalty and sacrifice. If you are traveling in England your opinion of that country is determined by your experience with the English. It rests with them more than it does with you. In the same, only in a more intensified way, because the Russian does not speak our language and knows little of our history or traditions, he must judge America on his own contacts with our people. The attitude he finally adopts for our country depends not so much on him as on what we Americans do to him.

**Industrial relations.**—After his first general impressions the next experience is in his job. Here he frequently does not meet with Americans at all, or if he does, it is merely for a formal question or two and for registration on the company's books. His real point of contact is with the boss. After talking with several hundred Russian workmen I found that ninety per cent or more fear and hate the boss. H. W. Anderson, City Secretary for Foreign Born in the New York City Y. M. C. A., says,

"The Russian comes to see America through the eyes of the saloon keeper, the paid politician, the partisan press and the propagandists. These all speak his language. He has never known what real patriotism is. He has ever thought of the government as an oppressor, and he transfers his mistrust, suspicion, and hate for the Russian government to the 'boss' where he works, who represents to him America. The 'boss' has not always been kind, and the Russian has embodied in his antagonism for him antagonism for America. A few days ago we witnessed a typical incident. Something had gone wrong with the work of some Russians. The men were not to blame, yet the young American foreman blamed it all on the —— —— lazy ——. They faced the angry tirade of the foreman with stolid, sullen faces and made no reply, yet in their hearts they registered one more case against America."

The Russians and Ruthenians frequently know few American words but they are all familiar with the common epithet the boss hurls at them, "You God damned Polack."

The disregarding of all racial distinctions simply accentuates the insult. The Russian soon learns that he is valued merely for his producing power. F. C. Howe, former Commissioner of Immigration at Ellis Island, says,[1] "because they have been broken down in the industrial machine . . . America refuses to assume the costs and consequences of its own industrial processes. It makes no provision for human depreciation, obsolescence or decay. It does this for its machines, but not for its human beings."

Many of the Russian priests claim their workmen get little or no compensation even in industrial accidents. They cite case after case of which the following is merely one illustration, from Father Kozuboff in Hartford who said, "In the hospital now there lies a man whose legs were crushed when a bucket for loading coal broke loose from the chain. The doctor says he can never walk, yet when he leaves the hospital he gets nothing, for he has no witnesses to the accident." Whether or not these statements are exaggerated, the Russian is a mere cog in the machine of production. Indeed he does not receive the care that parts of a machine do. They are constantly oiled and protected. Every possible care is taken of them, and when the machine is not in use a guard is kept on the premises. But for the human cog, little thought is taken. He can over-work, he can eat bad food, he can sleep in rooms ill-ventilated and unsanitary and the employer seemingly cares nothing. When the Russian "lays off" the job there is too often no human guard from the factory to see what can be done to help and protect him. If the cog is smashed to smithereens or even only injured so that he needs patching, the accident insurance covers the costs. The cog can be replaced immediately without cost by a new Russian or Ruthenian. If the machine is broken it means delay in production and new initial costs. In a large iron plant I visited in the summer of 1920 the doctor told

[1] *The Nation*, February 14, 1920.

me that an average of one-fifth of the working force visited the dispensary every month. "Most of them come from accidents to their eyes. We have not yet secured glasses which can be worn in the intense heat of the blast furnace," said he. Mr. Healy of the International Brotherhood of Stationary Fireman once went to the head of a great industrial corporation on behalf of their striking foreign workmen. That employer absolutely refused to consider an increase of pay. He said, "They are not worth any more to us; they are only cattle."

This brutal disregard of the human side of the Russian and Ruthenian is what they feel most keenly. As a common laborer, Mr. Whiting Williams, a warm-hearted employer, himself went into the steel mills and worked during the summer of 1919. When he came out he said, "The relation between the large employer and, for the most part, the foreign-born and foreign-speaking workers in the labor gangs" is expressed by the phrase of the workers, "Aw, w'at da hell! W'at da hell da companee care 'bout us?" Mr. Williams concludes that the astounding ignorance of the worker "concerning the plans and purposes, the aims and ideals, the character of the other human element in the same problem, his employer, is unequaled by anything I can think of—unless it is his employer's ignorance of him! To each the other stands as the 'X' in the equation of the factory organization. Of course; and who is most to blame, the ignorant Russian who does not even speak English, the product of an autocratic Tsar's government, continually abused by the boss, or the employer who has had every advantage that our boasted American liberty can give? Listen to Theodore Roosevelt as he lays the blame where it belongs: "Any employer who fails to recognize that human rights come first and that friendly relationship between himself and those working for him should be one of partnership and comradeship in mutual help no less than self-help, is recreant to his duty as an American citizen."

Furthermore, after the scare about Russian Bolsheviks had been widely flaunted by our press, the Russians began to be laid off right and left simply on account of their nationality. The inevitable result was that whereas these men had been good honest workers they became embittered and radical. This is expressed in a letter of an educated Russian from Worcester, Mass.: "Many thousands of Russians in this country while they work have hardly enough to live on, and now that the war is ended, they are discharged from factories, and told, 'you are a Bolshevik.' Many of them do not know what Bolshevism and what capitalism mean but they make real Bolsheviks out of them." Several large firms frankly told me that they refused employment to Russians. "We can get plenty of other nationalities," said one employer, "why take Bolsheviks?" Unfortunately from the standpoint of the Russian worker, it does not seem quite so fair. He comes to our country, works seven years in the steel plant, loses his best strength in the work and then is laid off because the Bolsheviks seize control in Russia. Can one wonder if some give up the struggle? On the bodies of two such Russians who were found dead on the railroad track, this explanation was found, "We prefer death to starvation. Have worked in the hell of a steel plant for seven years. Now they discharge us and we can't find a job."

During the recent steel strike the Russians stayed out loyally even after their meager funds had been exhausted. "We didn't start the strike," said one to me, "Americans are at the head of it. They told us that we would be traitors to our fellow workmen if we did not support the strike. Now we have done it for the sake of the others and the newspapers call us 'reds,' 'dogs,' 'I. W. W.'s.' " After the strike was lost, many of the firms refused to take back the Russians. One who was refused employment following the strike happened to have his apartment adjoining the steel plant. After two months' search he found a job in a mill one hour away from his home by street car. He worked eleven hours a day one week and thirteen hours a night the next. On his night shift fifteen hours were spent daily at his work and in traveling to and fro. It is small wonder that his wife was bitterly discouraged over the outlook. Yet the man had an American flag over his bed as well as a religious picture. His wife explained to me that when he can get away from his work he goes to church, and that before they had become disillusioned by the heartlessness of the corporations they had believed in America. Now she says, "We know America means money. We Russians are only like flies, too small—company doesn't care." I have talked with hundreds of Russian workmen and find their reactions to their industrial experience are much the same. Listen to what they say:[1]

"Before war, very good; but now all, no matter what nationality, laid off on least excuse. If horse no can pull wagon, put on another horse. If man no can pull truck, lay him off."

"Foreman very severe; sometimes lay off day for being minute late. Rush so at work that you almost faint. Treatment worse now since it is very easy to replace men."

"Boss very hard. Fired one man, he was in his place two minutes before whistle blew to enter shop."

"Bosses very unreasonable. One man left truck

[1] Some of these quotations are taken from Mr. Cole's Chicago study, others were spoken to me directly.

to get drink and boss fired him. Have to bribe boss to keep job."

"If he were good would not be boss. Boss like dog always snapping and swearing at everybody."

"Too strict about time; if one minute late, dock one-half hour. Getting worse all the time. Often work so hard get weak and when tell foreman he says we are drunk."

"All people treat Russian like dog."

"America place like Heaven for rich but like hell for foreign worker."

"America is not free for workers. He is beast like horse."

I realize perfectly that these are one-sided expressions. Part of the fault lies with the inherited traits and European background of the foreigner, yet they do indicate his psychological viewpoint.

The colossal profits made by the steel and coal companies are well known to the worker. He knows that the companies charge the public "all the traffic will bear" and it makes his arduous task and meager wage all the harder to bear. Statements such as McAdoo is reported to have made, that many of the coal companies made a thousand per cent profit during the war, are well known to many of the Russians and Ruthenians. Furthermore there is so much truth in the profiteering charges that they cannot merely be denied. The foreigner would refuse to believe it. He feels that he is the one who does the work and so is entitled to the profit. The actual fact of his bare subsistence wage in contrast to the profits of the concern makes his mind fertile soil for the work of clever American agitators. This actual industrial Americanization now going on is breeding a hatred for America and a contempt for our life. The worker characterizes it as a class rule for the benefit of the capitalist.

**Social relations.**—While industrial Americanization is doing its deadening work, the Russian's social relations in our country are paving the way for a still more distorted view of America. After his job, his impressions of America are next influenced by the little Jewish grocery and meat market on the corner from which he buys his food. There are few vegetables and what are obtainable are old and the storekeeper says that the exorbitant prices are due to capitalistic speculation. In giving the greatest need of the Russians to a government bureau, a Russian from Gary, Indiana, said, "We need fresh food products and fresh meat, and there is no such meat now in America." He spoke from his limited experience.

After an analysis of medical advertisements in Russian papers, Mr. Michael M. Davis of the Boston Dispensary, the head of the department on Health Standards of the Americanization Study of the Carnegie Corporation, says that they are "very obviously fakes." Here is a sample of one advertisement: "This is the only doctor from the old country."

"Fellow-citizens: look for help where you can find it, which will bring you out on the right path. This is the only doctor from the old country. He speaks Russian and has a practice of twenty-five years. He cures with the best remedies chronic and all diseases. Do not lose any time. Come promptly to his office. Advice free."

Naturally when the doctor once gets his hands on the Russian, the latter does not come forth until he has paid all that can be squeezed from him and sometimes he is heavily in debt. To the Russian the doctor is another side of America, which stands for money rather than friendship.

When the Russian has steady work and has saved something he must either keep it himself, which is dangerous, or bank it. So when he sees a large sign in Russian, "The State Bank," he hands over his money for safe keeping there. The Hon. C. J. Keenan, Deputy Appraiser of the Port of New York, said at a recent conference, "The people of foreign countries generally look upon a bank as a government institution, which accounts for the practice so prevalent among them of patronizing private banking institutions after they come to this country. An enterprising foreign-born citizen will oftentimes, after reaching a certain stage of prosperity, open a bank with the legend 'State Bank' over the door." Naturally whatever happens in this bank is attributed to the government. Usually the Russian does not receive any interest, he can feel fortunate if he ever gets his money back. Thousands and thousands of dollars are stolen annually—the banks simply disappear as do all the funds.

The Russian is a constant prey to exploitation. His rent may be raised at any time and the agent, representing wealthy Americans, is as likely to be a foreigner as an American. "When he is an American," as a Russian priest explained to me, "he is very polite as long as he thinks he can get your money. To illustrate this: one insurance agent crossed himself as he opened my door. After he received my order he went out slamming the door and spitting on the porch. Others come to see me to get the rent and they will offer me a cigarette, but if they don't have any business, they won't even talk with me and many of them won't recognize me the next day on the street—that is the soul of America." If to an educated priest this is the soul of America, what must it be to the poor, ignorant Russian.

Even the advertisements printed in the papers seek to exploit the Russian. In the *Russky Golos* during 1920 a corporation in a showy advertisement offered stock in a steamship company at $25 per share with the proviso that these shares could later be exchanged toward a steamship ticket to Russia which would cost from $125-$250. Yet a representative of a prominent social agency reported "that the investigation proves that the whole concern must be considered a fake one." The following is a sample of a patent medicine advertisement:

"Every Russian Mother knows that the only certain medicine for the crying and discomfort and sleeplessness of her baby is 'Romko' manufactured by the Baby Safety Company. Do not let your baby cry and suffer for hours. If your child has a stomach ache or suffers from constipation; if its teeth are coming and it is sick for this reason; if it cries and is discontented, do not wait one minute, but buy in the local drug store, for thirty-five cents, a bottle of 'Romko,' manufactured by the Baby Safety Company. If you cannot get the original there, send a paper dollar for three bottles, or stamps thirty-five cents for one bottle, to the following address:"

Thousands of dollars are likewise extracted from Russians in the process of sending money to friends in Europe. The recent revolution and war was made use of by clever manipulators who elected themselves "Aid Committees for Russian Sufferers." One of the priests showed me a very elaborate circular appealing for funds for suffering Russia, by which he claimed thousands had been raised and spent on the committee. The effect of every swindle can readily be seen in the following letter of a Russian:

"At first I believed in everything in America with an open soul. But in 1917 I decided to study automobiles. I paid $50 for a course and for this money I had the pleasure of riding in an automo-

# RELATIONS WITH THE AMERICAN PEOPLE 115

bile six times. There is much injustice going on, and without knowing the American law, one is always guilty."

Another Russian workman in California writes about his experience in trying to buy a farm in America. The first time he was swindled out of his money with a forged document. The second time a seemingly official "Russian-American agent" in Salt Lake City sold thirty-five Russian families land "and when we all arrived at the place we found a waterless desert. That is what is happening to the Russian people in America."

Even representatives of the Russian Orthodox Church have not been above some questionable methods. One of the priests told me that his predecessor borrowed from the workmen thousands of dollars to build a church on the promise that he would return the money as soon as the church was built. "Now the church is built," added the priest, "and of course I can't return any of the funds."

It is true much of this exploitation is done by foreigners, but the lamentable fact is that there are so few American agencies which are counteracting its evil effects. We have a few Americanization Committees, Y. W. C. A.'s and churches which are working to this end, but the results are almost infinitesimal compared with the need. The welfare work only reaches a fraction of the people a fraction of the time. Social contacts go on steadily day and night for every Russian. In this, the social side of their life, which could be made a real source of understanding normal American life, the Russian is meeting far too often merely exploitation or neglect.

### RELATIONS WITH GOVERNMENTAL AUTHORITIES

**Income tax.**—Undoubtedly the first place where the Russian and Ruthenian are touched today by the government, after they have gone through Ellis Island, is in the income tax. In regard to this law the Foreign Language Governmental Information Service Bureau of our Federal government says, "Many 'non-resident aliens' for instance, were taxed 12% of their gross earnings and allowed no exemptions, in spite of the provisions allowing exemptions to subjects of certain countries. It is neither necessary nor possible to go into details here. This bureau has complete records of thousands of aliens who were overtaxed."[1] This law provided a means of exemption for Russians, but there was no one to explain its provisions to the ignorant immigrant. Of one hundred employers only fifteen took the trouble to explain it to their employees in their own language. Yet after 1918 the government made the employer responsible for the collection of the tax and required the payment of back taxes. The injustice of collecting back taxes on eight per cent of the total income of a Russian workman is obvious. In some cases it amounted to from $50-$100. How was the Russian to meet his expenses during the period he was not receiving money from his employer? One letter out of hundreds to this bureau [2] from Russians will show the perplexity of even the educated ones:

"April 5, 1919.
"Natrona, Pa.

"I beg the Russian Bureau to help me. The Russian immigrants are not able to pay the war taxes. Some time ago I read in the papers that only those who earned more than $1,000 a year have to pay the tax and only on what they earned over $1,000, and I have paid $12.07. But now in the factory they

[1] From bulletin, *What is the Foreign Language Governmental Information Service Bureau?*
[2] Foreign Language Governmental Information Service Bureau.

## RELATIONS WITH THE AMERICAN PEOPLE 117

withhold more, and tell me that I myself have to pay $145 for last year, and if I have to pay for this year also, I will have to pay more than $300. And so I have to work, but do not get money to live on. And please explain why they force us to take out the American papers. Those who do not want to take the papers are put out of work. And if I take the papers will I be able to go back to Russia? And why did they put the Russian people in such helpless position? They do not allow us to return to Russia, and here it is now impossible to live.

"And I beg the Russian Bureau to answer my prayer, and tell me what is going to become of the Russian immigrants."

The attitude of some of the U. S. Internal Revenue officers is illustrated by the fact that the President of the Russian Society of Engineers in Chicago was refused an exemption blank by the officer until he forced the matter to the assistant Collector himself. He says, "The other Russians do not know where to get their rights and have to take out first papers, or pay enormous taxes." A government agent reports that in a large Ohio city "the Assistant Internal Revenue officer told me that he believed every Russian was a trouble maker; that since these Russians do not want to take out their first papers they should not be entitled to exemptions, that, furthermore, he did not consider it his business to instruct employees how to proceed with the various forms. From further talk with this officer I understand that no Russian will ever get justice if he applies to this office."

To illustrate still further the injustice of this law, take the Carnegie Steel Company. This firm employs about 10,000 Russians. They are entitled to tax exemptions if they fill out a sworn statement, but the company has found it easier to continue deducting the amount from wages. They have not the office force to handle these blanks and the inquiries which would result. A government agent reports, "These Russians decided that it is best to suffer injustice from the American Government than to ask or insist on their rights. Their previous experience, in matters of this sort has taught them a good and costly lesson. Their complaints are usually unheeded, and call forth new repressions." Hence the Russians continue to feel they are being cheated and the work of "Americanization" goes on.

**Laws against foreigners.**—The Russians and Ruthenians soon find that they are also discriminated against in the laws of the various states. I quote from the translation of an article which appeared in the Russian newspaper *Russki Slovo* on April 13th, 1920.

"Americans cannot understand why foreigners who have lived here for a certain time are in a hurry to return to their home. Here are some of the laws enacted against them: 'In the state of Nebraska, the foreigners have no right to have meetings except for religious purposes.

"In the state of Oregon, foreigners have no right to read newspapers and magazines which are not printed in English. The same law is proposed in the states of Maryland, Kentucky, and New York.

"In New Hampshire, the law forbids the employment of people between 16-21 years, if they do not know the English language.

"In the states of Michigan, New Hampshire, Tennessee, and Washington, foreigners have no right to teach.

"In the states of New York and Illinois the widows of foreigners have no right to the pensions allowed by law to American citizens.

"In the states of New Jersey, New York, Con-

# RELATIONS WITH THE AMERICAN PEOPLE

necticut, Washington, Nebraska, Kansas, Maryland, Oregon, and New Hampshire in case of accident, a foreigner does not receive the compensations which are due to American citizens in the same case.

"In the states of Pennsylvania, Illinois, New Jersey, California, Arizona, Rhode Island, Idaho, New Mexico, and Wyoming, foreigners cannot be employed on public works.

"In the state of Idaho a foreigner can be accepted for work in a factory only if he has his first citizenship papers.

"In the states of Illinois, California, Minnesota, Idaho, Texas, Missouri, Nebraska, Indiana, Montana, Arizona, Oklahoma, Kentucky, Iowa, Missouri, foreigners have no right to own property, or the ownership is limited between 5-20 years.

"If the work of the foreigner is appreciated, if he is needed in the mines and in the construction of subways and for works in factories and on farms, he must be given human rights and must not be offended at every step."

These laws may have some good purpose, but they do not make for friendship with the foreigner. They but continue the wrong type of Americanization.

*Arrests during strikes.*—Nothing has been written in recent times which so tellingly portrays the injustice of our present legal machinery as the bulletin of the Carnegie Foundation, *Justice and the Poor; a study of the present denial of justice to the poor.* In the introduction, after admitting the failure of our legal machinery to keep pace with legislation, it pleads for the equality of all men before the law and says: "For no group in the citizenship of the country is this more needed than in the case of the great mass of citizens of foreign birth, ignorant of the language, and helpless to secure their rights unless met by an administration of the machinery of justice that shall be simple, sympathetic, and patient. To such the apparent denial of justice forms the path to disloyalty and bitterness." The author of this study which has been highly praised by no less a legal authority than Elihu Root says in regard to the administration of justice: "You can work as hard as you like to teach the foreign-born resident to love American institutions, but if he doesn't get fair treatment when he comes in contact with those institutions, he will think they do not deserve his respect."

To any impartial observer of the facts, it is apparent particularly in a strike situation, that justice is not meted out to the Russian. Ordinarily thousands of special deputies are sworn in, and in the steel strike it was estimated that there were 3,000. Frequently these men are in the pay of the factory owners. The writer was a witness of conditions in the Lawrence, Massachusetts, textile strike. With a clergyman of New York he was forcibly ordered back off the public sidewalk simply because he dared walk by a mill; he saw the police ride upon the sidewalk following strikers peacefully walking on the streets. Although there was a state law permitting peaceful picketing, he heard a police officer who arrested Russians on strike swear in court that he knew of no such law. He saw the Russians come into the Union meetings with heads bandaged, claiming to have been arrested and beaten by the police. In the steel centers he heard tale after tale of oppression and brutality on the part of the police which, if true, rivalled the work of the Cossacks under the Tsar in Russia. Here are two Russians who attempted to go to another town in Pennsylvania during the strike. As they jump off the train they are arrested by two deputies with drawn revolvers and forced to pay a fine for vagrancy besides being banished from the town. Here is another Russian who claims the police came right into his house and arrested him without warrant after his foreman had begged him to return to work and he had refused. The Russian priest in Braddock told me that in a strike when two Russians were seen on the street speaking Russian they were arrested. Rev. Kazencz, a Ruthenian priest, testified before the U. S. Senate Committee that the constabulary charged on children who were in a school yard in sight of their parents in order to provoke the strikers to riot.

And so the incidents with their tragic aspect could be multiplied a thousand fold. Whether they are all true or not, the plain fact remains that many foreigners do not get justice in our law courts. They have not the money for lawyers' fees. The intrenched forces of law and order are naturally believed before the ignorant foreigner. But most of the Russians and Ruthenians who have passed through a strike believe the administration of justice to be a mockery. They are continuing their course in "Americanization" with the result that their opinion of America has been steadily falling.

Arthur Woods, formerly Police Commissioner of New York City, says in regard to Americanizing the alien that it is our American citizenship which is on trial. "There is no agitator in this world as potent as injustice. I often believe that there is no agitator of evil we need to fear except injustice."[1]

**Arresting "reds."**—The climax in the process of making America-haters out of our Russian foreigners came in the wholesale raids against "reds." Judge Anderson has sufficiently characterized the illegal and reprehensible methods employed by the U. S. Department of Justice. He says, "A mob is a mob, whether made up of government officials

[1] From an address in the Harvard Union, March 10, 1920. (*Harvard Alumni Bulletin*, p. 581.)

acting under instructions from the Department of Justice, or of criminals, loafers, and the vicious classes." A still more stinging report headed *"Illegal Practices of the United States Department of Justice"* was issued in May, 1920, by twelve eminent lawyers headed by Dean Pound of the Harvard Law School. It says, "Under the guise of a campaign for the suppression of radical activities, the office of the Attorney General, acting by its local agents throughout the country, and giving express instructions from Washington, has committed illegal acts. Wholesale arrests both of aliens and citizens have been made without warrant or any process of law; men and women have been jailed and held *incomunicado* without access of friends or counsel; homes have been entered without search-warrant and property seized and removed; other property has been wantonly destroyed; workingmen and workingwomen suspected of radical views have been shamefully abused and maltreated." The heaviest brunt of this illegal oppression has fallen on the Russian for he was supposed to have Bolshevistic leanings. Things reached such a pass that Francis Fisher Kane resigned as U. S. District Attorney while Judge Thompson of Pittsburgh, according to the newspapers, made the following comment on the case of a Russian brought to trial before him. "This case makes my blood boil. The methods of the Department of Justice have created more anarchy than all the radical parties put together and conditions in this district are worse than they were in Russia. I did not suppose this kind of thing could happen in a country where we have a constitution."

One can hardly realize the actual conditions without reading the actual cases. Theodore Concevich, of the Church of All Nations in New York City, says: "Joseph Polulech is a young Russian twenty-five years old. He was in America eight years. He

## RELATIONS WITH THE AMERICAN PEOPLE

was a member of the church and I was his pastor. He is a bright young man, eager to learn. He was attending a night school run by the Communist Party. He was studying English and algebra. He was not a communist, but he was made an officer in the school because of his faithfulness and intelligence. On the night that the school was raided by the Lusk Committee, everybody present was arrested, Joseph Polulech among them. I and others protested to the Lusk Committee and gave our guarantee that young Polulech was not a communist. We received no reply to our protest. Joseph Polulech is now among 249 aliens who are locked up in cars being pushed over the Finnish frontier." Mr. Concevich added, "Russians are now afraid to attend public meetings and classes for fear of having the police raid their meeting places and 'beat them up.'"

Mitchel Layrowsky, a teacher of mathematics, swore to the following: "I am 50 years old. I am married and have two children. I was principal of the Iglitsky High School for 15 years in Odessa, Russia. I declared my intention to become a citizen of the United States. On Nov. 7, 1919, I conducted a class at 137 East 15th St., New York. At about 8 o'clock in the evening, while I was teaching algebra and Russian, an agent of the Department of Justice opened the door of the school, walked in with a revolver in his hands, and ordered everybody in the school to step aside. Then he ordered me to step toward him. I wore eye-glasses and the agent of the Department of Justice ordered me to take them off. Then he struck me on the head and simultaneously two others struck me and beat me brutally. After I was without strength to stand up, I was thrown downstairs: and while I rolled down, other men beat me with pieces of wood, which I later found were obtained by breaking the banisters. I sustained a fracture of the head, left shoulder, and right side. Then I was ordered to wash myself and was taken to 13 Park Row where I was examined and released about midnight."[1]

Alexander Derkach testifies to the truth of the following:

"I was taken to a separate room and beaten up by one of the members of the Bomb Squad of New York City. He hit me on the head and twice in the stomach, and I fell senseless. I was taken to the lavatory and afterwards I was seated on the steps on the street—I fell down the steps—I walked away a distance of several blocks and fell down again. My friends came and carried me away."

The picture, opposite page 128, is an actual illustration of the condition of a room after the agents of the government had been through it.

In Duquesne, Pennsylvania, a professor of a government bureau lecturing on "Abraham Lincoln and American Democracy" to Russians was arrested and imprisoned as a Bolshevik because he lectured in Russian. It took the government thirty-six hours to free its own agent. He says, "After they found out who I was and set me free, I asked the mayor of the city whether he would allow me to deliver my lectures now. He said that he would not. I am convinced that no propaganda could be more effective in spreading animosity towards the American government."

The picture of the wife of a "Russian Red," page 32, in New Jersey shows a woman whose husband was kept in jail for three months and then released. In the meanwhile she had to live by means of the charity of her friends. The result of the "red" hysteria and threatened Bolshevik plots as given out by

[1] *Illegal Practices of the U. S. Department of Justice.*

the Department of Justice was that Russians everywhere suffered. The Greek Orthodox priest in Boston told me that things reached such a pass in his church that a crowd of Americans gathered and threw stones and tin cans at anyone who entered the church. Once he even had to get a policeman to conduct him from his home to the religious service.

It is small wonder that Russians or Ruthenians who have gone through conditions like these, do not love America. From their first impressions of our country down through their industrial and social experiences, through their relations with the government, they have not been in touch with the America that we know. This was strikingly shown in my experience. With the authorization of the Assistant Secretary of Labor, Mr. Post, I visited Russian prisoners in Detroit and Pittsburgh. Before this I had talked with Russians imprisoned at Ellis Island and Hartford. In my interviews I asked each Russian whether, during his stay in America, he had ever met any American who had helped him. I suggested that perhaps there had been some teacher, some boss, some boarding house keeper or worker who had been friendly to him. Out of nearly 150 arrested Russians there were only five who had ever met any such help. Of these American friends two had been workmen, two had been company doctors and one had been a teacher. On the other hand all the others had met many who had cursed them, foremen who called them "Russian swine," bosses who were continually swearing at them. America, according to their stories, had been for the most part one constant struggle against bad industrial conditions and exploitation. One could but feel that there was not so much bad in these men as there was in our American conditions which could force these people, helpless and needy as they are, to endure such treatment. They have seen where we are failing in our democratic ideal; they have seen our inconsistencies. It can hardly be considered their fault that Americanization to them spells the hardest toil, injustice, or unhappiness.

The following answers represent the spirit of America to a large number of Russian workmen and priests; they are surprisingly alike: "busy and business," "each help self," "rich man's land," "money," "love of self." One priest took me to the door and pointing to the mountain of coal dust and cinders at the mouth of the mine said, "That is the heart of America."

No one Russian would meet with all the misfortunes herein depicted; but the overwhelming majority have not seen the real America, the America that stands for justice, equality of opportunity, brotherliness. I believe that this real America is everywhere. Some of the Russians have tasted a little of its goodness,—those in North Dakota had a friendly hand extended to them in a time of need. Today they are loyal Americans, and no doubt there are thousands of others. Our task is to enable all the Russians even in our industries and mines to feel the warm, generous heart beat of our people that makes America dearer to us than any other land in the world.

The heart of America is sound if it can only be reached by the facts. It is the duty of the church to educate its membership on this question, to present the Christian solution, and to provide program and machinery for making the ideal real.

## Chapter VIII

## WHAT OF IT?

**A lull in immigration.**—Russian and Ruthenian immigration was practically stopped by the war. On account of the blockade on Russia, and the resulting unsettled conditions, its resumption has been prevented as far as these nations are concerned. This halted immigration is our God-given opportunity to organize our forces to help the vast army of Russians and Ruthenians who, in the years preceding the war, pressed in at such an irresistible pace that the Christian church was overwhelmed. This study has shown our defeat in the past; no one can predict what defeat in the future may mean.

**The future of the foreign language churches.**—Without incoming immigration, the foreign language churches will pass away. As the children of the Russian and Ruthenian are brought up in American schools, they forget the language of their fathers. Comparatively few of the second generation attend the foreign language churches and almost none of the third generation. Even one of the priests in the Orthodox church told me that if immigration should be stopped for one generation, his church would either have to be closed or readapt its service into the English. It seems probable that the halt in immigration is only the lull in the storm that predicts a still greater intensity. It would not be unlikely if the poverty and misery in Russia and Galicia should drive thousands more to this country. In the meantime our faces should be set to our present task.

**The church a force in racial assimilation and national unification.**—The Uniat and the Greek Orthodox Churches in the past can hardly claim to have been a force in racial assimilation and national unification. Their services have had to be conducted in the Russian language. Their priests have not themselves seen the best of America; they also have been isolated. On the other hand, the work of the Protestant churches has been woefully inadequate. The total Russian and Ruthenian members listed in the United States Census of Religious Bodies in 1916 being 6,997,[1] as compared with upwards of a million Russians and Ruthenians here. This was in 1916 and since then there has been a tremendous growth, but even in 1920 one of the leading Protestant denominations had, as its Russian minister told me, only two actual members although there were more on paper. According to the Russian pastor of another large church, the total Protestant membership in all New York City of all denominations does not exceed three hundred. The masses of these nationalities have been untouched.

Professors Jenks and Lauck, after their work with the United States Immigration Commission, wrote that Americans are almost completely ignorant and indifferent to the recent immigrants. "This attitude extends even to the native churches, and very few agencies have been established for the Americanization and assimilation of southern and Eastern European wage-earners. Not only is there a great field for social and religious work, but vast possibilities are offered for patriotic service in improving serious conditions which confront a self-governing republic." In spite of the advance which has been made in the work, this is almost equally true today.

[1] This includes thirteen mixed churches with a membership of 3,488.

SUNDAY MORNING IN A RUSSIAN HOME
"Whoso shall cause one of these little ones to stumble"
What chance have these Russian Children?                    [See page 46

THE RESULTS OF A RAID ON A RUSSIAN CLUB BY AGENTS OF "LAW AND ORDER"
"A mob is a mob whether made up of government officials or of criminals."
—JUDGE ANDERSON of Boston.

[See page 124

On page 64 is a picture of a group of Russians in Pittsburgh. They are the men who are doing the hardest work in our factories. The picture shows those Russians who took part in the Americanization parade on July 4th, 1918. Notice that nearly every man carries an American flag. Behind them are banners reading: "We Russian Workers Stand by President Wilson," "Yes, Greetings to the Soviet Federative Russian Republic." To the Russians then there was nothing necessarily incongruous in these banners—the one indorsing President Wilson, the other the Bolsheviks. What ought to be done with thousands of Russian and Ruthenian foreigners such as these? It was reported that what actually happened in this instance was the breaking up of the parade and the imprisonment of some of the flag bearers. Bolsheviks or brothers? There is only one Christian answer to that question.

**America needs the Russian and Ruthenian.**—Do we realize the debt we owe to the Russian and Ruthenian? We need them in our industries. A prominent manufacturer in Lawrence, Massachusetts, admitted to me that the textile mills would never be able to keep running were it not for foreign labor. "Americans would refuse to do the dirty work," was his comment. The U. S. Immigration Commission in 1909 [1] found in its investigation of 38 great industries that four-fifths of the operatives were either foreign-born or the sons of foreigners. The proportion would probably be still higher in 1920 for it has been since 1909 that the heaviest immigration has come, displacing still further American unskilled labor. Moreover, it is precisely in the essential industries such as iron and steel, coal mining, railway construction, meat packing, and sugar refining, that we find the Russian and the Ruthenian worker. Yet ex-President Wilson has said, "The

[1] Abstract of Report of Immigration Commission, Vol. 1.

welfare, the happiness, the energy and spirit of the men and women who do the daily work in our mines and factories, on our railroads, in our offices and ports of trade, on our farms, and on the sea, is the underlying necessity of all prosperity. There can be nothing wholesome unless their life is wholesome; there can be no contentment unless they are contented. Their physical welfare affects the soundness of the whole nation." But it is idle to pretend we have made our foreign workers happy and contented, least of all the Russians. Rabbi Wise of the Free Synagogue in New York City says, "I would have America either shut foreigners out or take them in, not leave them dangling in spirit at our doors, physically admitted to, but spiritually excluded from, the life of the Republic." The Russians and Ruthenians need the religious help of the church of the friendly Christ.

### RECOMMENDATIONS

**Coöperation.**—The results of our study reveal certain concrete steps which, in my opinion, should be taken. First, we should coöperate with the Russian Greek Orthodox Church. We do not want to proselytize. In every community where there is a Greek Orthodox Church our American churches should give every assistance that is welcome. This can best be done through the Episcopal Church which has had cordial relations of long standing with the Orthodox. It is not necessary, however, to confine such relationship to that denomination: any other church in the neighborhood could well do one or all of the following friendly things:

(a) Call on the Russian priest;
(b) Donate Russian New Testaments to him for distribution;

(c) Send gifts to the children's school;
(d) Lend a stereopticon or slides or both;
(e) Help in organizing a community service center in their parish for Russians.

My experience with the priests has convinced me that many of them would welcome coöperation from Protestant churches. Indeed some of the priests have said that they desired to be on friendly terms with the American churches but they must wait for them to make the friendly advances. Here is a chance for any of our city churches, particularly those located near the Russian districts, to help the foreigners. Now is a golden time to begin these friendly relationships for the Russian Greek Orthodox Church is financially embarrassed, no longer receiving support from Russia, and is losing its hold on its own constituency. The Independent churches which have broken away from the Greek Orthodox would be particularly glad to receive our help. Because of their activities in Russia and because many of the priests have felt that the Baptists were taking away their own members, it is probably true that that denomination would be the least successful in attempting such coöperation.

For the reason that the Uniat Church is under the control of Rome it is probable that such coöperation could not be as successfully established there as with the Russian Orthodox Church.

**Russian community institutional church.**—In the second place, in every city where there are large numbers of Russians there should be a Russian community institutional church. This should be located in the center of the Russian colony and ideally should have a definite educational, social and religious program besides a bureau of information and advice.

We have seen that the saloon has not yet been replaced by any wholesome agency. Today the Russian's total lack of a place to meet his fellows socially is pathetic. It is small wonder that one Russian working thirteen hours a night hopelessly exclaimed to me, "What crime have I committed that I should be compelled to live like this!" His life had not even the ray of hope that a friendly social agency brings. The community Church should meet this lack. It should have a tea room where the Russians could come at any time in the afternoon or evening for a social chat and a glass of tea. Russian communistic clubs had these facilities and they were very popular. This same tea room should be equipped with games such as checkers and chess, and Russian and English periodicals and papers. Where possible the church should also have a gymnasium and shower baths with an instructor to teach gymnastic drill and games. A doctor on part time, at least, and a visiting nurse could do a wonderful work, not only in relieving suffering but in teaching prevention and the laws of health. A moving picture outfit with educational and recreational films would be indispensable. This could show the best side of American life to the Russians as well as help to amuse and entertain them. For example, American methods of farming, athletics, pictures of American homes, our higher institutions of learning, historic buildings, all would be of incalculable value in teaching him American ideals.

The children's work of the church should all be coördinated under a paid director of religious education and should include a school of religion, boy scout work, and various other clubs.

We have seen how the Russians have been exploited. They patronize fake doctors, they do not always get justice in our courts, they need advice in regard to flats and tenements, they often lose money in accidents and employment, they pay unnecessary income taxes and they need advice on a thousand and one matters, such as the best banks to deposit money in, passport difficulties and so forth. To meet these needs such a church should have a Bureau of Information and Advice. This should be under a competent Russian, or an American speaking the language.

The Russian longs for education; his own blundering efforts in this direction have been broken up and prohibited by the police. The church should have a definite educational program with English and arithmetic classes, practical courses in agriculture, automobile-driving and manual training. There should be a library of Russian and American books and lectures on hygiene, American ideals, history, science, and other subjects.

Permeating all this work should be the religious motive. We cannot expect to win the Russian for Christ unless we care as Jesus cared for men. If we tell the Russian and Ruthenian of Christian principles and ask him to become a follower of the Master and yet make no effort to Christianize the environment in which he works, how can we expect him to remain a Christian? The tragic truth is, as we have seen, that the Protestant churches of New York City which are working among the Russians have pitifully few active members. If, instead of a so-called exclusively religious evangelistic work, we adopt the institutional church idea for the Russians, we shall grip their whole lives. Rather than making converts among those who are simply inclined to be fanatical, we shall make converts among all types of Russians and we shall also be making a genuine attempt to be brothers to all. Such an institutional church would include all the religious activities of the evangelistic church: preaching, Bible classes, and the rest. It should have an American in charge and at least two Russian assistants.

The total budget for such a work would vary, of course, with the place, the extent of the program, and the number reached. Specimen work, however, could undoubtedly be started, exclusive of original equipment, on a minimum of $1,000 per month. This would pay for an American minister, at a salary of $250, and a Russian staff of two men at $150 each. The Russian People's Institute now secures a building in New York City for $200 a month. This would leave a balance of $250 a month for other assistants, equipment and up-keep.

It is apparent that each individual denomination could not afford to start a large plant, perhaps not even at the minimum figure suggested above. If, however, all those denominations who are interested in Russian work would join in such a central community institutional church, it could easily be done. In that case, the religious services could all be united and carried on under a single head or they could be continued separately by the present denominational method but the social and educational work and information department could be conducted jointly. In any case, there should be an interdenominational board for Russian work representing all churches doing work in a given city for the Russians. Where it was not possible to unite on either of the above plans it would still be able to eliminate friction from rivalries and church barter for Russian workers. At present if they are discharged by one denomination they may be engaged at once by another, or if they do not get sufficient salary with one, may go to another. Eventually it may even prove possible for each denomination doing work for Russians to be assigned a certain geographical district in the United States as is done in the mission field and so make the results more effective.

Where there are not large Russian colonies it may be necessary to include other nationalities in this plan. Many of them, no doubt, need help almost as much as the Russians. In the big Russian centers such an institution ought to be for Russians alone. It could never be so successful when appealing to a polyglot of tongues and races because of the differences in racial psychology. The difference is vividly brought home if we think of which would make the stronger appeal to us in Paris, an American community church or only a polyglot foreign center with an occasional English sermon. Not only should the church adopt a consistent, constructive program, but also the government and those industries in which foreigners are employed. If the church takes the initiative in a broad, adequate movement for Russians, she will undoubtedly stimulate wholesome changes in governmental and industrial activity. In any event, she will act as a clearing house for all the work for Russians in the city, thus tending to coördinate all these agencies.

The Ruthenians do not need help as much as the Russians. They attend their churches better, they seem to have more social organizations, and, since Russians and Ruthenians do not mix well, where possible the community institutional church should be wholly Russian with a separate Ruthenian plant. Where this is impossible it might be practicable to have merely a Ruthenian department.

**Hospitality.**—In the third place, every Protestant American church now located in a Russian district should not rest until it has a Russian group meeting within its doors. Perhaps the easiest way to accomplish this is to make friends with the leaders of the common Russian workmen in that district and offer to let them use the church rooms freely. They should be permitted to organize themselves in their own way, to find out what they need by themselves and do what they wish. If they care to have lectures favorable to Bolshevism occasionally and discussions on the present conditions in Russia these should be permitted because only so will they be willing to hear lectures opposing Bolshevism. Gradually, as they come to have faith in the purpose of the minister, they will be glad to accept English teachers and other lectures. Eventually it ought to be possible to have a paid Russian worker added to the staff, and if the experience of other Protestant churches is worth anything some of the Russians will eventually join the church. Moreover such hospitality would unconsciously tend to make every American church member hold out a friendly hand to the Russians he met in the common places of everyday life. If every church now located in a Russian district would extend a cordial welcome to their alien brothers in this way it would go far toward Americanizing and Christianizing the Russian.

**Religious and secular literature.**—In the fourth place, we need adequate religious and social literature for the Russians and Ruthenians in their own language. This should be specially prepared for the needs of today. It should deal with his experiences in factory, mill, and tenement. Too often we have used tracts and religious thought-forms of a bygone age. Jesus was constantly speaking in terms of his own time. How much could be done if all the denominations would unite in printing joint Russian Bible study books, a joint religious periodical and general literature! This could be prepared in Russian under the supervision of an expert.

**The trained expert.**—In the last place, every denomination having extensive Russian work should include on its staff an American having had some experience in Russia and speaking the language. It would be his task to travel from center to center where Russian colonies are to organize and direct the work. Similar men should do a similar work for the Ruthenians. None of our denominations would think of trying to maintain missionaries on the foreign field with no training and with no knowledge of the language. Yet so often we attempt work among the Russians without having even a single American familiar with their language, to say nothing of the European background and life out of which they came.

The issue.—In this study we have seen something of the needs of the Ruthenians and Russians. The questions raised by Dr. Coe in his *A Social Theory of Religion* are surely pertinent here: "If one human life outweighs a world, as Jesus taught, what should we do with a social order that stunts multitudes of human lives for the sake of money, and does it, not by disobedience to the laws of the state, but under the protection of laws and courts? How can we really believe in human brotherhood, if we are willing to acquiesce in a stratification of society into the servers and the served, the rulers and the ruled?" Burke says, "To make us love our country, our country ought to be lovely." Doubly true it is, if we would inspire in the foreigner this same love.

We have tried to outline a concrete program to meet the needs of our foreign brothers. It is not complete, it is only the first step, but the needs call loudly for action. The Russian is only one part of the gigantic task before the Christian forces of America in the immigration problem alone. These foreigners come offering all that they have,—to our industries, the strong bodily physique which God has given them; to our communities, their inherent racial gifts. What shall we offer in return? Shall it be friendliness or indifference? Whether they shall be Bolsheviks or Brothers rests rather with us than with them.

Appendix A

# BIBLIOGRAPHY

*Russia*

### GENERAL BOOKS

BAEDEKER, KARL—*Russia*—Scribner, 1914. The best tourist guide to Russia.
BARING, MAURICE—*Russian People*—Doran, 1911.
BUBNOFF, I. B.—*Coöperative Movement in Russia.* —M. Fainberg, N. Y., 1917.
FANNING, C. E.—*Russia*—H. W. Wilson Co., 1918. A useful compilation of magazine articles on the historical, descriptive and political aspects of Russia. It also includes a good bibliography.
GRAHAM, STEPHEN—*The Way of Mary and Martha.* A popular sympathetic treatment of the religious side of Russia.
KOVALEVSKY, MAXIME—*Russian Political Institutions*—University of Chicago Press, 1902.
MILYUKOV, PAUL—*Russia and its Crisis*—University of Chicago Press, 1907.
RAPPOPORT, A. S.—*Home Life in Russia*—Macmillan, 1913.
VINOGRADOFF, PAUL—*Self Government in Russia.* —Dutton, 1915.
WALLACE, D. M.—*Russia*—Holt, 1905. The *Review of Reviews* says, "It is regarded by many Russians as the best work about their country ever written by a foreigner."
WALLING, W. E.—*Russia's Message*—Knopf, 1917.

WILLIAMS, H. W.—*Russia of the Russians*—Scribner, 1914. One of the best brief books on Russia.

U. S. DEPT. OF COMMERCE (Special Consular Report No. 61)—*Russia: a handbook on commercial and industrial conditions* by J. H. Snodgrass, 1913.

### RUSSIAN HISTORY

BEAZLEY, FORBES, AND BIRKETT — *Russia* — Oxford Press, 1918.

HOWE, S. E.—*A Thousand Years of Russian History.*

KLUCHEVSKY, V. O.—*History of Russia*—3 vols. Dutton. Probably the best and most authoritative Russian history.

KORNILOV, ALEKSANDER—*Modern Russian History*—Knopf, 1917.

SACK, A. J.—*The Birth of the Russian Democracy*—1920. The Russian Information Bureau. Traces the revolutionary movement in Russia down to the present time.

### THE RUSSIAN CHURCH

REV. R. W. BLACKMORE, Translated by the—*The Doctrine of the Russian Church*—Joseph Masters & Co., 78 New Bond St., London.

BEAULIEU, LEROY—*The Empire of the Tsars and the Russians*—Vol. III, Putnam, 1896. Although old it is probably the best book on the religious movement in Russia.

LACEY, T. J.—*A Study of the Eastern Orthodox Church*—New Edition, 1912.

MOURAVIEFF'S—*History of the Russian Church.*

STANLEY, DEAN—*The Eastern Church*—Everyman's Edition.

HAPGOOD, I. F.—*Service Book of the Holy Orthodox-Catholic Apostolic Church*—Houghton Mifflin & Co., 1906 (at present out of print).

## BIBLIOGRAPHY

### RUSSIAN LITERATURE

BARING, MAURICE—*Landmarks in Russian Literature*—Macmillan, 1910.
BRUCKNER, A.—*Literary History of Russia*—Scribner, 1908.
HAPGOOD, ISABEL F.—*Survey of Russian Literature, with Selections*—1902.
KROPOTKIN, PETER—*Ideals and Realities in Russian Literature*—Knopf, 1915.
PHELPS, W. L.—*Essays on Russian Novelists*—Macmillan, 1911.
WIENER, LEO—*Anthology of Russian Literature*—2 vols. Putnam, 1903.

### RUSSIAN ART AND MUSIC

BENOIS, ALEXANDRE—*Russian School of Painting*—Knopf, 1916.
HOLME, CHARLES—*Peasant Art in Russia*—Lane, 1912.
MONTAGU, NATHAN M.—*Contemporary Russian Composers*—Stokes, 1917. Also *History of Russian Music*—Scribner, 1914.
NEWMARCH, ROSA — *Russian Arts* — Dutton, 1916. Also *Russian Opera*—Dutton, 1914.
SAYLER, OLIVER M.—*The Russian Theatre*—1919.

### IMMIGRATION: GENERAL

ADDAMS, JANE—*Twenty Years at Hull House*—Macmillan, 1910.
COMMONS, J. R.—*Races and Immigrants in America*—Macmillan, 1908.
DAVIS, PHILIP—*Immigration and Americanization*—Ginn, 1920.
FAIRCHILD, HENRY PRATT—*Immigration*—Macmillan, 1914. One of the best standard books.
JENKS AND LAUCK—*The Immigration Problem*—Funk & Wagnalls—1911, and revised 1917.

## 142  RUSSIANS AND RUTHENIANS IN AMERICA

Based very largely on the Report of the Immigration Commission of 1910. An excellent book.

HOURWICH, ISAAC A.—*Immigration and Labor*—G. P. Putnam Sons, 1912. Largely statistics. Opposes restriction of immigration.

KELLER, FRANCES A.—*Straight America*—Macmillan, 1916.

ROBERTS, PETER—*The New Immigration*—Macmillan, 1912.

ROSS, E. A.—*The Old World in the New*—Century Co., 1914.

STEINER, E. A.—*Immigrant Tide*—Revell, 1909.

WARNE, FRANK J.—*The Tide of Immigration*—Appleton, 1916.

### IMMIGRATION: RELIGIOUS ASPECTS

BROOKS, C. A.—*Christian Americanization*—1919. Missionary Education Movement.

GROSE, H. B.—*Aliens or Americans*—1912. Missionary Education Movement.

SHRIVER, W. P.—*Immigrant Forces*—1913. Missionary Education Movement, New York.

MCCLURE, ARCHIBALD—*Leadership of the New America*—1917. Doran, New York.

MARY CLARKE BARNES and LEMUEL CALL BARNES—*The New America*—1913. Revell, New York.

STEINER, E. A.—*On the Trail of the Immigrant*—1906. Revell, New York.

### THE RUSSIANS IN AMERICA

AINSWORTH, F. H.—*Are We Shouldering Europe's Burden?* (Charities), Feb. 6, 1904, v. 12, pp. 134-135.

BALCH, EMILY G.—*Our Slavic Fellow Citizens*, New York Charities Publication Commission, 1910.

BOAS, FRANZ—*Race Problem in America* (Science—1909, v. 29, pp. 839-49).

BOECKH, RICHARD—*The Determination of Racial Stock among American Immigrants* (American Statistical Association Quarterly Publication, Dec., 1906, pp. 199-221).

BYINGTON, MARGARET F.—*Homestead; The Households of the Milltown*, 1910, 292 pp.
An intensive study of 90 households in Homestead nearly one-third of which were Slavic. In 1907 when the mill of the U. S. Steel Corporation was running at full capacity 53.2% of employees were Slavic.

*California Commission of Immigration and Housing, Report of Fresno's Immigration Problem*, State Printing Office, Sacramento, 1917.

*California Commission of Immigration and Housing, Report on an Experiment in Los Angeles in summer of 1917 for Americanization of Foreign-born Women*, State Printing Office, Sacramento, 1917.

CANE, ALEXANDER E.—*Slav Farmers on the "Abandoned Farm" Area of Conn.*, Survey, Oct. 7, 1911.

CLAGHORN—*Immigration in its Relation to Pauperism* (annals of the American Academy, July, 1904, v. 24, pp. 207-20). *Our Immigrants and Ourselves* (Atlantic, 1900, v. 36, pp. 535-48).

COMMONS, J. R.—*Race Composition of the American People* (Chautauquan, September, 1903-May, 1904).

COMMONS, J. R.—*Slavs in the Bituminous Mines of Illinois* (Charities), Dec. 3, 1904, v. 13, pp. 227-29; (also) Industrial Commission, v. 15, pp. 293-743, 1901.

COMMONS, J. R.—*Wage Earners of Pittsburg* (Charities, March 6, 1909, v. 21, pp. 1051-64).

ELKINGTAR, JOSEPH—*The Doukhobors; their Character and Economic Principles* (Charities, 1904, v. 13, pp. 252-56).

Dimock, Leila Allen—*Comrades from Other Lands* (Subject: Slavs in Industry), Revell Co., 1913.

Fitch, John A.—*The Steel Workers*, Pittsburgh Survey, 1910.

Fleming, W. L.—*Immigration to the Southern States* (Pol. Science Quarterly, 1905, v. 20, pp. 276-97).

Foster, Maximilian — *The Citizen* (Everybody's, Nov., 1909).

Grose, Howard B.—*The Incoming Millions*, 1906. (The Slavs are treated separately in the chapter on "The Immigrants in Their New Home.")

Henry, John R.—*Some Immigrant Neighbors* (Subject: Our Russian Neighbor), Revell Co., 1912.

Hodges, Le Roy—*Slavs on Southern Farms*, Sen. Doc. 595, U. S. 63 Cong. 2 Sess., Wash. Gov. Printing Office, 1914.

Hrdlicka, Ales—*The Slavs* (Czecho-Slovak Review, Nov., 1918, v. 2, pp. 180-87).

Kellogg, Paul W.—*The McKee's Rocks Strike* (Survey, Aug. 7, 1909, v. 22, pp. 656-66), *Protection of Immigrant Women* (Atlantic, 1908, v. 101, pp. 246-55).

Lee, Joseph—*Assimilation and Nationality* (Charities, 1908, v. 19, pp. 1453-55).

Lloyd, J. A. T.—*Teuton versus Slav* (Fortnightly Review, May 1, 1916, New Series, v. 99, pp. 883-93).

Lovejoy, Owen R.—*The Slav Child: A National Asset or a Liability* (Charities, July, 1905, pp. 882-84).

McClure, Archibald—*Leadership of the New America*, Racial and Religious (Part II, Immigrant Leadership among the Slavic European Nationalities), Doran, N. Y., 1916.

McLaughlin, Allan—*The Slavic Immigrant* (Popular Science Monthly, May, 1903).

# BIBLIOGRAPHY

Mayo-Smith, Richmond—*Theories of Mixtures of Races and Nationalities* (Yale Rev., v. 3).

Miller, H. A. (Survey, June 15, 1919, v. 40, pp. 307-09).

Norton, Elliott S.—*The Need of a General Plan for Settling Immigrants Outside the Great Cities* (Charities, Feb. 6, 1904, pp. 152-54).

Parker, E. H.—*Russians in Business*, Chamber's Jl., Feb., 1915, pp. 103-06. (Their unbusinesslike methods.)

Prugavin, Aleksander Stepanovich—Several Pamphlets in Russian on *Russian Religious Sects* in N. Y. Public Library.

Prugavin, A. S.—*Die Inquisition der Russisch-Orthodoxen Kirche. Die Klostergefängnisse.* Berlin. F. Gottheiner, 1905, 124 pp.

Ripley, Wm. Z.—*Race Factors in Labor Unions* (Atlantic, 1904, pp. 299-308). *Races in the United States*, 1908, 102 pp.

Roberts, Peter—*Immigrant Races in North America*, 1912.

——. *The New Immigration*, 1913.

Ross, E. A.—"The Slavs," Chap. 6 of *The Old World in the New*, 1914, p. 327.

*Russians in America* (Literary Digest, Nov. 29, 1919, p. 41).

Sayles, Mary Buell—*Housing and Social Conditions in a Slavic Neighborhood* (Charities, Dec. 3, 1904, pp. 257-61).

Sheridan, Frank J.—*Italian, Slavic, and Hungarian Unskilled Immigrant Laborers in the United States* (U. S. Labor Bulletin, No. 72, 1907).

*Slavic Alliance in Cleveland.* Cleveland, 1904. (In Russian.)

Smith, Robert K.—*The People of the Eastern Orthodox Churches*, Springfield, Mass., 1913, p. 20.

SMITH, RUFUS D.—*Some Phases of the McKee's Rocks Strike* (Survey, Oct., 1909, pp. 30-35).
SOKALOFF, ALEXIS—*Medieval Russia* (Pittsburgh Survey).
SOKALOFF, A.—*Old Believers* (Survey, Nov., 1914, v. 33, pp. 145-50).
SOKALOFF, LILLIAN—*Russians in Los Angeles.* University of Southern California, March, 1918, p. 16—Soc. Monograph, No. 17.
STEINER, EDWARD A.—*From the Lovczin to Guinea Hill* (Outlook, May, 1908).
STEINER, E. A.—*The Broken Wall* (Subject: A Slavic Oklahoman), Revell Co., 1911, N. Y. and Chicago.
TOWNLEY, FULLAM C.—*Pan-Slavism in America* (Forum, Aug., 1914, pp. 177-85).
TOYNBEE, A. J.—*The Slav Peoples,* Polish Quarterly, Dec., 1914, pp. 33-68.
*United for Freedom at Home* (Survey, June, 1908, p. 292).
VAN KLEACK, M.—*Russians in the Flower Trade,* N. Y. Survey Association, 1913.
WARNE, F. J.—*The Coal Mine Workers,* 1905; *The Slav Invasion and Mine Workers,* 1904.
WARNE, FRANK J.—*Immigrant Invasions,* Chap. III, Invasion of Slavs and Italians; Chap. VI, Some Economic Characteristics of the Immigrants; Chap. VIII, Standards of Living, part Slavs and Italian. Dodd, Mead & Co., 1913.
WING, M. T. C.—*The Flag at McKee's Rocks* (Survey, Oct., 1909, pp. 45-46).
WOOLSTON, FLORENCE—*Slavs in the U. S.* (Technical World, Oct., 1911, pp. 135-44).
WRIGHT, CARROLL D.—*Influence of Trade Unions on Immigrants* (Bulletin of the U. S. Bureau of Labor, 1905, No. 56, pp. 1-8).

## BIBLIOGRAPHY

IMMIGRANTS IN INDUSTRIES (Subject: *Slavs in U. S.*), Wash. Gov. Print. Office, 1911; 61 Cong., 2 Sess., Sen. Doc., v. 68-85.
*Russians in United States* (also Slavs), U. S. Immigration Commission, v. 5; *Dictionary of Races and Peoples*, 61:3d., v. 9, pp. 111-18.
*Slavs in United States,* U. S. Immigration Commission, 61st Cong., 3 Sess., Sen. Doc., v. 7.

## Appendix B

## THEOLOGICAL SEMINARIES

FOREIGN LANGUAGE THEOLOGICAL SEMINARIES AND OTHER INSTITUTIONS TRAINING RUSSIAN STUDENTS FOR THE MINISTRY AND OTHER CHURCH WORK.

BALDWIN-WALLACE COLLEGE (Slavic Dept.), Berea, O.
BERKELEY BAPTIST DIVINITY SCHOOL, Berkeley, Cal.
BLOOMFIELD THEOLOGICAL SEMINARY, Bloomfield, N. J.
BROADVIEW THEOLOGICAL SEMINARY, La Grange, Ill.
CHRISTIAN BIBLE COLLEGE, Minneapolis, Minn.
CROZER THEOLOGICAL SEMINARY, Upland, Pa.
DUBUQUE COLLEGE AND SEMINARY, Dubuque, Ia.
EUGENE BIBLE UNIVERSITY, Eugene, Ore.
FISK HALL (Non-denominational), Chicago, Ill.
INTERNATIONAL BAPTIST SEMINARY, E. Orange, N. J.
INTERNATIONAL Y. M. C. A. COLLEGE, Springfield, Mass.
MISSION HOUSE SCHOOL, Plymouth, Wis.
MOODY BIBLE INSTITUTE, Chicago, Ill.
NEWTON THEOLOGICAL INSTITUTE, Newton Center, Mass.
NORTHERN BAPTIST THEOLOGICAL SEMINARY, Louisville, Ky.
RUSSIAN BIBLE INSTITUTE, Philadelphia, Pa.
RUSSIAN ORTHODOX THEOLOGICAL SEMINARY, Tenafly, N. J.
SOUTHWESTERN BAPTIST THEOLOGICAL SEMINARY, Fort Worth, Tex.

## Appendix C

## RELIGIOUS PERIODICALS: RUSSIAN AND UKRANIAN

### RUSSIAN

*Amerikansky Russky Viestnik*, weekly, Thurs., Gk. Cath. Union, Homestead, Pa.
*Golos Tzerkvy* (*Voice of the Church*), bi-weekly; REV. PIOTROWSKY, Editor, 628 Grant St., Pittsburgh, Pa.
*Key to the Truth*, monthly, Bible and Tract Society, 13-17 Hicks St., Brooklyn, N. Y.
*Nedelye*, F. N. BARKETAFF, Editor, Russian Orthodox Clerical League, 347 E. 14th St.
*Norodny Poychenia* (issued irreg.), Bible and Tract Society, 13-17 Hicks St., Brooklyn, N. Y.
*Pravda* (*Truth*), Semi-Weekly, E. K. HOYNIAK, Editor, 213 N. Willow St., Olyphant, Pa.
*Russbrlhodoy* (*Voice of the Church*), REV. S. BAZELEVICH, Editor, International Printing Co., 628 Grant St., N. Y., Pittsburgh, Pa.
*The Friend of Russia and Revivalist*, WILLIAM FETLER, Editor, 1844 W. Monroe St., Chicago, Ill.
*The Sower of Truth*, Monthly, J. DAVIDUK, Editor, 1014 Main St., Hartford, Conn.—"A Religious Union Christian Monthly."

### UKRANIAN

*Prawda*, Bloomfield Seminary, Bloomfield, N. J.
*Prosvita* (Greek Catholic) (Enlightenment), Prosvita Pub. Co., McKeesport, Pa.
*Ranok* (*Morning*), Weekly (Presby.), Union Press, Winnipeg, Can.
*Sojuz* (*Union*), Weekly (Thurs.), 1001 Manufacturers Bldg., Pittsburgh, Pa.

# INDEX

Accidents in industry, 107.
Addams, Jane quoted, IX, 65.
Advertisements intended for immigrants, 114.
America needs the Russian and Ruthenian, 129, 130.
American leadership imperative, 102, 103.
American mind, learning, 71.
American people, relations with, Chap. VII, 104-126.
Americanizing influences, 102, 105.
Americanization in the public schools, 59; the parochial schools a force against, 60; Russian newspapers, a force for or against, 64; parade on July 4, 1918, 129; real, 105.
Anderson, Harvey, quoted, 66, 106.
Anderson, Judge quoted, 121.
Arizona laws, 119.
Arresting Russians and Ruthenians during strikes, 120-121; for political offenses, 121-124.
Assimilation: agencies in, 68-74, 128.

Baptists in Russia, 81; in America (Russians), 84; Ruthenians, 84.
Banks for the immigrant, 113.
Bolsheviks and Bolshevism: 49, 65; all Russians treated as, 73, 97, 109, 120; individual instances, 122, 123.
Budget for community church, 134.
Bull, *Magnus Dominus*, 75.
Burke quoted, 137.

California laws, 119; immigration commission, 68.
Carnegie foundation bulletin quoted, 119-120.
Children's work, 31, 32.
Chicago, annual report police department 1919, 50; report of Chicago City Council Committee on Crime 1915, 50.
Church of Christ in America (Russian), 84.
Church a force in racial assimilation and national unification, 128.
Coe, G. A. quoted, 137.
Cole, G. S., Chicago study of 1919, 10, 33, 35, 36, 37, 43, 70, 71.
Communist clubs, 54, 61, 65.
Communist and Coöperative experiments, 82.
Constructive social forces, 56.
Coöperation with the Greek Orthodox Church, 131-132.
Connecticut laws, 119.
Creel, George, quoted, 67.
Criminal statistics, 49.

Davis, Michael, health standards quoted on housing, 41, 112.
Davis, Philip: immigration and Americanization, 56.
Denominationalism, 101.
Denominational foreign language training schools, 99, 100.
Detroit, prisoners visited in, 125; Ford employees' housing, 39, 40.
Devine, Dr. Edward T., *Family and Social Work* quoted, 32.
Disciples of Christ (Russian) in America, 84, 85.

# INDEX

Economic conditions, Chap. II, 27-38.
Educational forces, Chap. IV, 58.
Ellis Island, 104, 105, 107, 125.
European background, 19.
Evangelism, 86.
Exorbitant costs—food, 34.
Exploitation, 105, 113, 114, 115, 132.

"Fact of God," the, 89-90.
Faiths, old-country faiths and churches retained, 75-79.
Family groups, 24.
Family life, 46, 47.
Fanatical sects, 82, 87.
Fanatical tone of Russian religious periodicals, 88.
First impressions of the immigrant, 104.
Food, typical fare of the Russian workman, 35, 43.
Forces, destructive social, 54.
Ford plant, statistics of welfare department, 39, 40.
Foreign- and native-born occupations, 27-28.
Foreign language governmental information bureau, 61, 66, 116; training schools, 99-102; used in training, 99; churches, future of, 127.

Governmental authorities, relations with, 119, 121, 122.
Greek Catholic church, 75.

Hayden, Rev. Joel B., 98.
Health, 42.
Hecker, Dr., 94.
Hourvich, Dr., quoted, 21.
Hospitality in Protestant churches, 135-136.
Housing, 39-42.
Howe, F. C. quoted, 107.

Idaho laws, 119.
Ikon, 78.
Illinois: Russians in, laws, 119.
Immigration, Chap. I, 21, 22; a lull in, 127.
Income tax, 116-118.
Industrial relations, 20, 106-111.

Indiana laws, 119.
Iowa laws, 119.
Industries, in which Russians and Ruthenians are found, 27-28-29; need Russians and Ruthenians, 129.
Information, bureau of, in Community Church, 131, 133.
Institutional church, 85; Russian Community Institutional church, 131-135.
Interdenominational Foreign Language Training school, 100-101.
International Baptist Seminary, 100; efforts, 100, 134.
Inter-Racial Council, 21, 23, 64.
Isolation of Russian students, 100.
"Ivan," case of, 30-31.

Jenks and Lauck quoted, 128.
Jews, 20, 47-48, 51, 52, 55, 88, 112.
"Justice and the Poor," bulletin of Carnegie Foundation, 119-120.

Kane, Francis Fisher, quoted, 122.
Kansas laws, 119.
Kinsmen trained in America, 94-95; trained in their native land, 93-94.
Kentucky laws, 119.

Labor unions, a force in assimilation, 68.
Lawrence, Mass., incident in, 120; conditions during strike, 120-121.
Laws against foreigners, 118-119.
Leadership, 64-65.
Learning the American mind, 71.
Letters from Russians, 73.
Libraries, their use by Russians, 60.
Literacy among Russians and Ruthenians, 69, 70.
Literature and newspapers, 60-64; religious, 88; general, 88, 92; needed, 136.
Los Angeles, 39.

# INDEX

Maryland laws, 118, 119.
Means of livelihood, 27.
Method of investigation, IX-XI.
M. E. Church (Russian) in America, 84, 86.
Mennonites (Russian) in America, 101.
Methodists in Russia, 81.
Michigan laws, 118.
Migrations in the United States, 24.
Miller, Rev. Kenneth D., 98.
Minister of Kin, 87.
Minnesota laws, 119.
Missouri laws, 119.
Missionary work in Russia, 81.
Monotony of labor, 24, 31, 47.
Montana laws, 119.
Moral standards, 49-50.
Moving pictures, 44.

Naturalization, 71.
Nebraska laws, 119.
Neighborhood life, 47-48.
New England Russian population, 22.
New Hampshire laws, 118, 119.
New Jersey laws, 118.
New Mexico laws, 119.
New York: laws, 118; Russians in, 22.
Newspapers, Russian, 61; quotations from, 62-64.
Nicholas, Bishop, quoted, 78.
North Dakota, 29, 30, 48.
*Novi Mir* suppressed, 61; quotation, 62.
Number of Russians in America, 20-24.
Number of Russian and Ruthenian workers in different industries in the United States, 27-28.

Ohio, Russians in, 22; colonies, 30.
Oklahoma laws, 119.
Old believers, 80.
Omelchenko, E. I., quoted, 21.
Oregon laws, 118, 119.
Overcrowding, 35.
Owners of homes, 39.

Pennsylvania: laws, 119; Russians in, 22.
Periodicals, religious. See Appendix.
Petrunkevich, A., quoted, 68, 70.
Philadelphia, 98.
Pittsburgh: housing, 40-42; prisoners visited in, 125-126; Americanization work in, 66; wages in, 33.
Polyglot Community church, 133-135; Training schools, 101-103.
Pound, Dean Roscoe, and report of twelve eminent lawyers, 122.
Presbyterian church (Russian and Ruthenian) in America, 84.
Press, secular, 88; religious, 88-89.
Producers in the family, 36.
Progress in Protestant work since 1916, 84.
Prohibition amendment, effect of, 44.
Protestant church affiliation, 84.
Protestant Episcopal church (Russian and Ruthenian) in America, 84.
Protestant work done, 94, 95.
Proverbs, Russian, 77.

Racial prepossessions, 53.
Rauschenbush, *Social Teachings of Jesus*, 91.
Recommendations, 130-137.
Relation to the old country, 50; to other racial groups, 50.
Relations with the American people, Chap. VII, 104-126.
Religious approach, forms of, 85-87.
Religious break-up, forms of, 78-83.
Religious Conditions, Chap. V, 75-92.
Religious nature of the Russian people, 76-78.
Religious press, 88.
Religious realignments, forms of, 84.
Rents, 33, 34, 40.
Return movement, 25, 26.
Rhode Island laws, 119.
Roosevelt, Theodore, quoted, 108.

# INDEX

Russian Bible and Educational Institute, 93.
Russian and Ruthenian defined, 19, 20.
Russians and Ruthenians in the U. S., 22, 23.
Russian and Ruthenian children in the public schools, 58-59.
Russian Collegiate Institute in New York City, 68.
Russian Educational clubs and reading rooms, 56.
*Russki Golos*, 61, quoted, 62.
*Russki Slovo*, 61, quoted, 36, 63, 64, 118.
Russian Greek Orthodox church, 56, 59, 60, 75-83, 103, 131; future of, 127; coöperation with, 94, 130, 131; growth of the democratic spirit, 83; questionable methods, 115; split in America, 78, 82; training priests in America, 94; Russian priests needing sympathetic help, 104.
Russian People's University, 69.
Ruthenians in U. S., number of, 24.
Ruthenians, distribution of, 23.

Salaries of Russian pastors, 95.
Saloon, 44, 55.
Savings, 36, 37.
Schools: the public, 58; parochial, 59.
Schismatics and sectarians, 80-83.
Sears, Dr. Charles H., on Baptist work in America, 85.
Secular press, 88.
Seminary, Baldwin-Wallace, 100.
Services held in the Russian, Ruthenian and Slav languages.
Seventh Day Adventists (Russian) in America, 84.
Shriver's *Immigrant Forces* quoted, 97, 99.
Single men (migrations), 24, 34.
Social conditions, Chap. III, 39-57.
Social and industrial training of leaders, 91, 95.
Social needs, 137.

Social organizations and forces, 54-57.
Social relations, 112.
Social settlement, 85.
Sokaloff, Lillian, "The Russians in Los Angeles," 39.
Soldiers, treatment of, after the war, 72.
Soldiers' wages (Russian) in late war, 19.
Standards of living, 33-35.
Steiner, E. O., quoted, 55.
Steel strike, 109, 110.
Stundists, 29-30, 81.

Tennessee laws, 118.
Texas laws, 119.
Theological seminaries, 100.
Tolstoy, Count, 79, 81.
Training of foreign-born Russian ministers, 94, 99.
Tracts, 89-92; recommendations for, 90-91.

Uniat church, 75, 128, 131.
United States census, 20; census of religious bodies, 1916, 84, 128; immigration commission, 27, 28, 29, 32, 33, 35, 39, 49, 58, 59, 67, 69, 71; labor department, 33.
Unrest, 37.
Use of languages, 69-70.
Use of racial sentiment, 70.

Vilchur, M., *The Russians in America*, quoted, 22, 36.
Virginia colonies, 29.

Wages, 32-33.
War service, results reflected from, 72.
Washington laws, 119.
What of it? Chap. VIII, 127-137.
Williams, Whiting, incident from, 108.
Wilson, President, quoted, 38, 130.
Women social workers, 98.
Woods, Arthur, quoted, 121.
Wyoming laws, 119.